ONE WEEK LOAN

EDMUND SPENSER
from a portrait at Pembroke College, Cambridge
reproduced by kind permission of the Master and Fellows

Edmund Spenser

Colin Burrow

Northcote House

in association with
The British Council

First published in 1996 by Northcote House Publishers Ltd, Plymbridge House, Estover Road, Plymouth PL6 7PZ, United Kingdom.
Tel: +44 (0) 1752 202300. Fax: +44 (0) 1752 202330.

British Library Cataloguing-in-Publication Data
A catalogue record for this book is available from the British Library

ISBN 0 7463 0750 0

Typeset by PDQ Typesetting, Newcastle-Under-Lyme
Printed and bound in the United Kingdom

Contents

Preface   vi

Biographical Outline   vii

Note on the Text   x

1   The Biographical Record   1

2   A Renaissance Poet   11

3   Dynastic Epic   27

4   Allegorical Epic   43

5   Heroes and Villains and Things in Between   55

6   Wild Men and Wild Places   72

7   Love and Empire   80

Appendix. *The Faerie Queene*: Summary   101

Notes   107

Select Bibliography   109

Index   117

Preface

This very little book deals with a very big author. It might be helpful to say briefly what goes on in it. The first two chapters cover Spenser's life and shorter works, with the exception of the *Fowre Hymnes* and the *Amoretti*, which are considered in the last chapter. The next five deal with some of the more major questions which arise from the breathtaking complexity of *The Faerie Queene*. These chapters approach the poem thematically rather than sequentially, but the majority of examples in Chapters 3 and 4 come from the first three books of the poem. Chapters 5, 6, and 7 range more widely, but shift their attention towards the second three books of the poem. These later chapters are a shade more difficult, too, since the issues which they address take me into some of the more complex areas in a very complex poem. The Mutabilitie Cantos, which were published after Spenser's death, are discussed under several headings. They reflect on so many of the areas which Spenser was exploring in the rest of the poem that I found the best way to deal with them was to approach them from several angles. At the back of the book there is a summary of the main actions in *The Faerie Queene* to assist those who have not read, or who cannot remember, all of it. Notes have been kept to the barest minimum, often, I fear, to the extent of being rude to the very many scholars to whom I owe debts. I hope that in the Select Bibliography I have done something to redress the balance.

I would like to thank Gavin Alexander and J. A. Burrow for their expert scrutiny, and Miranda for being so tolerant of the many occasions on which I was in the loft writing it when I should have been somewhere else. And, although it is a small book, I would like to dedicate it to her with love.

Biographical Outline

1552–4   Born, probably in London, probably to John Spenser, a
          clothier, and Elizabeth.
1561   Attends Merchant Taylor's School, probably from its
          foundation (20 Sept.).
1569   Matriculates at Pembroke Hall Cambridge, as sizar (20
          May). *A Theatre for Worldlings* entered in Stationers'
          Register (22 July).
1570   Friendship with Gabriel Harvey begins.
1573   Takes his BA, graduating 11th out of 120 candidates.
1576   Takes his MA, graduating 66th out of 70 candidates.
1577   Possibly in Ireland, where he may have witnessed the
          execution of Morrogh O'Brien (1 July).
1578   Becomes secretary to John Young, Bishop of Rochester
          (Apr.). In London, dwelling at Mistress Kerke's (by
          Dec.).
1579   Dwelling at Leicester House, probably as secretary to the
          Earl of Leicester, by 5 Oct. Marriage of 'Edmounde
          Spenser to Machabyas Chylde' at St Margaret's,
          Westminster (27 Oct.). Two children: Sylvanus and
          Katherine. *The Shepheardes Calender* entered in
          Stationers' Register (Dec.). Printed soon after.
1580   Lord Grey appointed Lord Deputy of Ireland (15 July).
          Spenser his secretary, on £20 p.a. Spenser almost
          certainly present at the siege of Smerwick, followed by
          the massacre of its 600 defenders (Oct.–Nov.). Spenser–
          Harvey correspondence printed (Dec.). Second edition
          of *The Shepheardes Calender*.
1581   Becomes Clerk to the Controller of Customs on Wines
          (22 Mar.). Granted lease of a Friary and Mill at

	Enniscorthy, Co. Wexford (6 Dec.).
1582	Obtains lease of New Abbey, Co. Kildare, for £3 p.a. (24 Aug.). Lord Grey recalled to England (31 Aug.). Spenser remains in Ireland.
1583	Appointed Commissioner for Musters in Co. Kildare (12 May).
1584	Probably becomes Clerk of the Council of Munster, serving as deputy to Lodovic Bryskett (July).
1586	Third edition of *The Shepheardes Calender* (17 Dec.).
1588	Possibly begins to occupy Kilcolman Castle (definitely in occupation by 24 Mar. 1589). Quotations from *The Faerie Queene* appear in Abraham Fraunce's *Arcadian Rhetorike*.
1589	Legal disputes with his Old English neighbour, Lord Roche (Oct.). Familiar with Ralegh, and travels with him to England, to supervise the publication of *The Faerie Queene*, which is entered in Stationers' Register (Dec.).
1590	*The Faerie Queene* printed. *Complaints* entered in Stationers' Register (Dec.).
1591	*Daphnaïda* printed. Granted life pension of £50 p.a. (25 Feb.). Returns to Ireland. Fourth edition of *The Shepheardes Calender*. *Complaints* printed; 'Mother Hubberds Tale' possibly suppressed. *Colin Clouts Come Home Againe* dated (27 Dec.). Continued disputes with Lord Roche.
1592	*Axiochus*, a translation of a pseudo-Platonic dialogue attributed, probably wrongly, to Spenser.
1594	Further disputes with Lord Roche (Feb.). Marries Elizabeth Boyle (11 June). One son, Peregrine.
1595	*Colin Clouts Come Home Againe* printed. *Amoretti and Epithalamion*, 'written not long since', printed.
1596	*Fowre Hymnes* printed. *A Vewe of the Present State of Ireland* composed, possibly while in England (June–July).
1597	Fifth edition of *The Shepheardes Calender*.
1598	*Vewe* entered in Stationers' Register, but not approved for publication (14 Apr.). In arrears with rent (7 Feb.). Tyrone rebellion breaks out (June). Spenser made Sherriff of Cork (30 Sept.). Kilcolman falls to the rebels (Oct.). Returns to London. Paid £8 for delivering a letter to the Privy Council.
1599	Dies (13 Jan.) in London. Buried at the charge of the Earl

of Essex.
1609   First folio of *The Faerie Queene*, including the Mutabilitie
        Cantos.
1611   First folio of collected poetical works.
1617   Second folio of collected poetical works.
1620   Funeral monument erected in Westminster Abbey.
1633   Publication of *Vewe*.
1679   Publication of first collected edition of verse and prose.

Note on the Text

All quotations for *The Faerie Queene* are taken from the edition by A. C. Hamilton (Longman Annotated English Poets; London, 1977). Quotations from Spenser's shorter poems and their prefatory and dedicatory material are from *The Yale Edition of the Shorter Poems of Edmund Spenser*, ed. William A. Oram *et al.* (New Haven, Conn., and London, 1989). Quotations from *A Vewe of the Present State of Ireland* and *Three Proper, and Wittie, Familiar Letters* are from *The Works of Edmund Spenser: A Variorum Edition*, ed. Edwin Greenlaw *et al.* (10 vols.; Baltimore, 1932–57), vol. x, *The Prose Works*, ed. Rudolf Gottfried (Baltimore, 1949). In quotation from early sources modern practice has been adopted with regard to i/j and u/v, with the major exception of quotations from *The Faerie Queene*. This is because, as modern editors of the poem accept, the effects of Spenser's language are often more clearly visible in an old spelling text. Names of characters in *The Faerie Queene* have been regularized in my text, and the forms I have given are not always those most frequently used by Spenser. 'Arthegall' is more often called 'Artegall' by Spenser; but the former is used here since it brings out Spenser's suggestion that the knight of Justice is the equal of Arthur. 'The Redcrosse Knight' is called 'Redcrosse' only once, by his Lady Una. Her familiar, abbreviated, form of the name has become an accepted norm, and so is used here.

1

The Biographical Record

Edmund Spenser's tombstone (to begin at the end of his life) stands as a warning to would-be biographers:

HEARE LYES (EXPECTING THE SECOND
COMMINGE OF OUR SAVIOUR CHRIST
JESUS) THE BODY OF EDMOND SPENCER,
THE PRINCE OF POETS IN HIS TYME;
WHOSE DIVINE SPIRRIT NEEDS NOE
OTHIR WITNESSE THEN THE WORKS
WHICH HE LEFT BEHINDE HIM.
HE WAS BORNE IN LONDON IN
THE YEAR 1510. AND
DIED IN THE YEARE
1596.

Erected in 1620 by Anne Clifford, Countess of Dorset, and daughter of one of the dedicatees of the *Fowre Hymnes*, the monument gets all but one of its facts wrong. If we are to believe the 'witnesse' of Spenser's *Amoretti* 60, he was 40 in 1594, so was born in about 1554. He died on 13 January 1599, failing to creep over the threshold of the new century. He was, though, probably born in London, since the *Prothalamion* calls the city 'my most kyndly Nurse, | That to me gave this Lifes first native sourse' (ll. 128–9).

The monument is revealing about Spenser, however, in its very sparseness. It was carved by James I's wonderfully named master mason, Nicholas Stone, who was later to produce the extraordinary memorial of John Donne, in which the poet is depicted in his shroud with the face of death upon him. Spenser's monument is, by contrast, undemonstrative, and as chilly as only tombstones can be. Where Donne left a mass of familiar letters, and poems which reach out and command with an intimately abrupt directness, neither Spenser's monument, his life

1

records, nor his verse leave much of the texture of the man behind. Most of the evidence about his life falls into two categories, both of which need to be treated with some care. The first includes his own statements in poems and proems about his career. These tend to be pictures of how Spenser would have wished to be thought of, rather than of how he was. The second group includes official documents – records of leases and appointments and so on – which again need cautious handling. They present the material dimension of Spenser's career, his financial and legal self, to the exclusion of all else. No one looks attractive if one considers only his or her bank statements. Spenser's life is to be found somewhere between those two kinds of source.

The records of Merchant Taylor's School show that Spenser was educated there, and that he received an allowance for a mourning gown in 1569. This is consistent with the hypothesis that his father was a clothier of slender means. Elizabethan grammar schools had a way of making poor scholars know that they were poor scholars; but they also had a remarkable record of taking poor scholars, grinding Latin, and, in the higher forms, Greek and Hebrew, into them from 7 to 11 a.m. and from 1 to 5 p.m. every day, and turning them into major writers. Spenser's headmaster was Richard Mulcaster, who wrote eloquently and reasonably about education, and who was an advocate of expanding the range and raising the importance of the vernacular. He also had an interest in darkly allegorical writing. While still at school, and probably under the influence of Mulcaster, Spenser translated a number of sonnets by the French poet Joachim Du Bellay for the Protestant Jan van der Noodt's collection of poems and woodcuts, *A Theatre for Worldlings*. The apocalyptic zeal of the volume, and its militantly anti-papal stance, had a lasting influence on Spenser.

In the same year, 1569, Spenser went up to Pembroke Hall Cambridge as a sizar (a poor scholar who did domestic tasks to pay his way). At Cambridge he studied rhetoric, logic, and philosophy, as well as music, astronomy, geometry, and mathematics. His time there overlapped with one of the hottest theological controversies of the period, that between Thomas Cartwright and John Whitgift in 1570. Cartwright, the new Lady Margaret Professor of Divinity, argued for radical reform of the Elizabethan Church in order to bring it into line with the primitive church described in Acts 1 and 2. This would involve the abolition of the name of bishop and archbishop, leaving only those of pastor and deacon. He raised eager support among the younger generation at the University, and was eventually expelled from his chair by the manœuvrings of John Whitgift, later Archbishop of Canterbury. Cartwright's views may have had an influence on Spenser's advocacy of pastoral simplicity in *The Shepheardes Calender*, and could have built on the anti-papal Protestantism of *A Theatre for Worldlings*.

At Cambridge, Spenser met Gabriel Harvey, a querulous and sporadically learned son of a wealthy rope-maker. Harvey became a fellow of Pembroke Hall in 1570, and praelector in rhetoric in 1574. His loyal colleagues, no doubt maddened by his windy ambition (some of his best prose describes how earthquakes are produced by a build-up of subterranean wind), attempted to prevent his taking an MA. Harvey's life ended obscurely in Saffron Walden, after he had lost his fellowship and been savaged by the pen of Thomas Nashe. But in the 1570s he appeared to be an energetic reformer, who was a champion of the new logic of the French educator Ramus (Pierre la Ramée). It is likely that Spenser spent much of the years 1574–8 (which is a period of his life about which we know very little) in Harvey's company, possibly in his intimate company. The two read books in bed together, and, in *The Shepheardes Calender*, the character Hobbinol, who is an unmistakable image of Harvey, is vainly in love with the poet Colin Clout.

The connection with Harvey makes the years 1578–80 the best documented in Spenser's life. In 1579 Harvey almost certainly collaborated in the publication of *The Shepheardes Calender* – and he might even be the eclectic and pedantic mind behind EK's notes to the volume (other candidates are Spenser himself, or an otherwise little-known fellow of Caius called Edward Kirke). In 1580 appeared *Three Proper, and Wittie, Familiar Letters with Two Other, Very Commendable Letters* (Elizabethan title-pages seldom sold themselves short), which contain, interspersed with replies, excursuses from the replies, and excursuses from the excursuses by Harvey, the only 'familiar' letters of Spenser to survive. The letters yield a few facts: that Spenser was dwelling at 'Mistress Kerke's' in London by the end of 1578, that he was at the house of the Earl of Leicester in 1579, and was in the service of Leicester,

3

probably as a secretary, by that year. The letters also enthusias-
tically record that he met Sidney and Dyer at Leicester House, and
that he conferred with them over the best means to introduce
classical 'quantitative' verse (that is, verse in which scansion is
based on the length of syllables, rather than on stress or accent)
into English. They also insinuate that Spenser may have met the
Queen, and excitedly mention works by Spenser which do not
survive (his *Dreames* 'full as great as my *Calender*' the *Epithalamion
Thamesis*, a marriage song of the Thames, which at least one
witness read in Latin, *The Dying Pellicane*, and what was
presumably to have been a genealogical poem about the Earl of
Leicester, the *Stemmata Dudleiana*). Taken together, these 'facts'
are too good to be true: the letters are suspiciously keen to sing
the praises of their authors, to inflate the canon of their works,
and to present Spenser as the virtual laureate poet of the Earl of
Leicester, who was the most powerful patron of letters in the
period. The introductory epistle to the letters claims that they
came to the printer as a result of a piece of well-meaning piracy by
an anonymous friend; but it is hard to believe that Spenser and
Harvey did not assist in their publication. Such adroitly faked
pseudo-piracy was a favourite trick of George Gascoigne, another,
more established, poet in the circle of Leicester. Spenser had
recently published *The Shepheardes Calender*, and Harvey was
seeking to become Public Orator of Cambridge, so both figures
needed to extend their reputations. The letters are also designed
to give their readers the illicit pleasure of eavesdropping on an
exciting and mildly conspiratorial reform of English verse. The
group of Sidney, Dyer, and Spenser is referred to as the
'Areopagus', the parliament (effectively) of Athens, and they
describe their activities in political, and specifically parliamentar-
ian, terms ('they have by authoritie of their whole Senate,
prescribed certaine Lawes and Rules of Quantities of English
sillables, for English verse'). Lacing the letters are conspiratorial
requests to keep each others' writings 'close'. Only two elements
in them can be corroborated from external sources. The first is the
earthquake, about which Harvey windily expands, which did
shake London on 6 April 1580. The second concerns the walk-on
part accorded in them to 'Collyna Clouta', with whom Spenser is
supposed to be in love. This may just be a joke about the obsession
of Spenser's own persona in *The Shepheardes Calender*, Colin Clout,

4

with Rosalind. But it gives some reason to suppose that the marriage recorded between Edmund Spenser and 'Machabyas [i.e. Maccabaeus] Chylde' on 27 October 1579 at St Margaret's Westminster, was that of the poet.

Spenser was not, of course, a full-time poet. He pursued the career to which his education best suited him: that of an administrator. Elizabethans who were not nobly born, but who were well educated, could go into the law, or the church, scratch a living by writing, or act as personal secretaries to noblemen, or highly placed churchmen. In 1578 Spenser followed this last course, and became secretary to John Young, Bishop of Rochester. He probably then became secretary to the Earl of Leicester in 1579. It has been thought that some disagreement with Leicester (to which Spenser darkly alludes in the preface to 'Virgils Gnat') may have led him to be effectively banished to Ireland in 1580. In *The Shepheardes Calender* he may allude to Lettice Knollys, whom Leicester secretly married in 1578, in an unguarded way ('And learne with Lettice to wexe light' ('March', l. 20) which means 'become wanton'); but Ireland was a place in which many ambitious Elizabethans who could not find a job in England tried their luck. For whatever reason, it was in Ireland that Spenser spent most of the rest of his life, as a colonial administrator and landowner. He probably had only two extended periods in England after 1580. Between 1589 and early 1591 he came across with Ralegh in order to oversee the printing of *The Faerie Queene*, and of the *Complaints* volume. This led to his being granted a magnificent pension by the Queen of £50 p.a. for life. In 1595–6 he is thought to have come across once more to oversee the printing of the second instalment of *The Faerie Queene*. But by 1595 'home' to him meant Ireland. On 11 June 1594, in Ireland, he married Elizabeth Boyle.

Ireland in the 1580s and 1590s was a province on the brink of rebellion, occupied by three mutually hostile populations. It contained the native Irish, the so-called 'Old English' (mostly the descendants of noblemen who had occupied Ireland under William the Conqueror), and a new generation of ambitious colonial administrators, often of strongly Protestant views, who regarded themselves as the people who would finally render Ireland subject to English law. These men, of whom Spenser was one, were tasked with subduing and earning a living from the

Irish. One of the principal means for doing this was by 'planting' – that is, by leasing large areas of land from the Crown at good rates, and then establishing self-contained agrarian communities on them. These ventures were hazardous: it was extremely difficult to prove good title to the land which one was granted, and the native Irish and Old English were increasingly hostile to the New English. Sir Thomas Smith's much publicized plantation of the Ard in 1572 serves to illustrate some of the dangers faced by would-be planters. The scheme was not funded adequately by the Crown, and the inhabitants were understandably outraged by the invasion of English entrepreneurs who claimed to possess their land. The efforts of Smith's son, also called Thomas, to run the plantation had a grim end: he was eventually boiled in a pot and fed to the dogs by his household servants.[1]

Spenser started his Irish career as secretary to Lord Grey, the Lord Deputy of the province. This was more than a clerical job: it required Spenser to follow Grey in the field in his campaigns against the rebels, and in his efforts to suppress Spanish infiltrations of Ireland. In October 1580 Spenser almost certainly witnessed the massacre of a predominantly Italian, but Spanish-backed, garrison at Smerwick. Six hundred soldiers had surrendered to Grey, who killed them all, and, according to some reliable reports, tortured men and killed women. Grey claimed that he had secured an unconditional surrender, and so could justifiably treat his captives as he wished. Rumours, though, and strong ones, suggested that the surrender was not unconditional, and that Grey had at least hinted that he might spare his captives. His massacre may have been an act of illegality as well as of singular inhumanity. Despite this, Spenser was to become a vocal defender of Grey's reputation.

Grey's violent style of government did not find favour with the Crown or the Privy Council in England, and he was recalled in the summer of 1582. With Grey's departure, Spenser, after a brief period of un- or under-employment, took on the less lucrative but less dangerous post of deputy to the Clerk of the Council of Munster. He probably received this office by the gift of his friend Lodovic Bryskett in July 1584. It required his attendance at the Irish parliament, and gave him continual direct experience of the legal business of the region. The legal tangles faced by planters would have been a daily preoccupation, and a nightly bad dream for him.

Spenser made money out of the province, some of it, in all likelihood, less than cleanly. There are regular disparities in the amounts he received to disburse to messengers, and the sums he actually paid out. This does not necessarily indicate that the surplus found its way into Spenser's pocket, since his duties might well have included paying spies, the records of which might be expected to be as invisible as their recipients; but there is a smell of graft to it. He secured the rewarding post of Clerk to the Controller of Customs on Wines, won the leases of largish properties at Enniscorthy and in County Kildare, and eventually secured, at £20 p.a., the lease of Kilcolman Castle and its lands. This was an estate of around 3,000 acres in the south-west of Ireland. Spenser had continual boundary disputes with his Old English neighbour Lord Roche. These were regular occurrences for New English settlers, who were not welcomed by the Old English nobility. But it is also likely that Spenser was guilty of making his boundary posts walk by night, and of provocative incursions into his neighbour's lands by day.

By 1596 – the year in which Books IV–VI of *The Faerie Queene* were published – Spenser had completed *A Vewe of the Present State of Ireland*. This was a radical statement of the desires of the New English. It lists instances in which the English common law conflicted with Irish customs, and advocates a potent mixture of legal reform and the suppression of Irish customs in order to end the incompatibility. It is unrelentingly hostile both to the Irish and to the Old English. At the centre of the *Vewe* is a radical demand to send over an army of crack English troops to complete the utter subjection of the Irish 'even by the sword'. The province should be beaten and starved into submission, then divided into self-supporting units, each of which would have its own English garrison. Like many works written in support of the policies of the New English, the *Vewe* frequently uses agrarian metaphors to describe the process of imposing Englishness on Ireland: the verb 'to plant' is used of laws, customs, and of garrisons. Growing food, cultivating *mores*, and killing people were seen by the New English as closely interwoven activities. The *Vewe* represents a latter-day real-life version of Thomas More's *Utopia*. It displays all of More's wish to reorganize society, and all his lawyer's sensitivity to the role of custom and precedent in determining human conduct. But, unlike the mild fantasies of More's narrator

Hythloday, those of Spenser's spokesman Irenius require mass extermination in order to realize them, and issue in military rule. The *Vewe* is strikingly aware of the contingency of civilizations, of how their customs unfold, and of the possibility of refashioning them. It is also a work of cold brutality.

Spenser's plans were never realized. The ambitions expressed in the *Vewe* ran directly counter to royal policy on Ireland (which, like most aspects of Elizabethan foreign policy, was in favour of scant action and even scantier expenditure). It was not printed until 1633, despite Spenser's efforts to get it past the censor in 1598. In 1598 Spenser was either proved terribly right or horribly wrong about Ireland. Tyrone's rebellion, led by troops trained on the English model, swept the province. The rebels sacked Kilcolman and drove Spenser home to London, where he died in the early days of 1599. Ben Jonson reported that he died in poverty, and that in the fire which destroyed Kilcolman there perished 'a litle child new born'.[2] No other witness corroborates this, and Jonson's claims look very like projections of his own concerns onto Spenser, since the most powerful single theme in Jonson's verse is the death of children. It is also very unlikely that Spenser died in poverty. A payment of £8 made to the poet for carrying letters from Ireland shortly before his death makes it unlikely that he 'died for lake of bread in King Street', as Jonson reported in 1618–19; but it may well be that he died despairing over the failure of his life in Ireland.

Much of the best recent criticism of Spenser has related his poetry to his experiences in Ireland. His life does draw one's eye suspiciously to both the violence and the fragility of the missions enacted by the allegorical heroes of *The Faerie Queene*. Their conquests of demonized passions, their repeated encounters with ghostly starving figures, and their overall goal of fashioning a cultivated self from the wilds of an allegorical world, all refract into fiction the attempts of an English planter to bring what he saw as cultivation to what he saw as a barbarous nation. There are also fascinating parallels between the Irish bards, whom Spenser presents in the *Vewe* as creating a mythology suited to resistance and rebellion, and Spenser's own writings, which create a mythology suited to conquest and control. Ireland is frequently the twin of Spenser's English imaginings, and, as we shall see, the later phase of his career shows a New Englishman acquiring a near-native concern for the land, and an uneasy affinity with the savage. But to read the earlier works of Spenser through the hard prism of the *Vewe* itself can lead to distortion. It was probably (with the exception of the *Prothalamion*) the last work Spenser wrote. It marks the end of a period of fear and of growing frustration with the wavering, penny-pinching policies of his Queen. It is where many of Spenser's earlier writings are heading, but it is not always where they were.

Spenser is often talked and written about as though he were the quintessential court poet, who wrote flattering poems to his Queen from a secure position near the centre of Elizabethan authority. This may be how his poems are (although this book will suggest a rather different view of them), but it is not how his life was. True, he held a substantial pension of £50 p.a. for life after the publication of *The Faerie Queene*. But in general his relations with the centres of power were far from easy, and his poetry is not simply to be identified with Elizabethan orthodoxies. In his works there are two significant portraits of a poet: the first is Colin Clout, who sings laments in *The Shepheardes Calender*, and whose praises of the 'Queene of Shepheardes' Eliza have to be sung for him by his friend Hobbinol. This is because Colin, rather than musing continually on his Queen, is mourning his frustrated passion for Rosalind. Colin Clout returns in 1595 to attack the practices of the court in *Colin Clouts Come Home Againe* – and 'Home' in the title means, not England, but Ireland. His final appearance in Spenser's works is a tantalizing glimpse in Book VI of *The Faerie Queene*, in which the knight of Courtesy, Sir Calidore, sees the poet having a solitary vision of the Graces. The poet is pointedly removed from a political environment: he is a poet of loss, exile, and solitude.

The other major portrait of a poet in Spenser's works is that of Bonfont, who is portrayed on the threshold of Mercilla's court in *The Faerie Queene*, V. ix. Bonfont's original name ('fountain of goodness') is erased by an unnamed force of punishment, and is replaced by 'Malfont' ('fountain of badness'). His tongue is nailed to a post, for slandering his Queen. Spenser never suffered as Bonfont did, but his works did not have an easy relationship with the censor. Several of Spenser's contemporaries (including Harvey) record that 'Mother Hubberds Tale', a beast fable about an ape and a fox which was printed in the *Complaints* volume of

9

1591, offended the Queen's chief minister Lord Burghley for its outspoken criticisms of the ways in which highly placed courtiers could assume and manipulate royal authority (the ape steals the lion's royal regalia in the satire). These witnesses have it that attempts were made to suppress the volume. Book V of *The Faerie Queene* inspired the rage of James VI of Scotland for its hostile portrayal of his mother, Mary, Queen of Scots. The poem was suppressed in Scotland, and James desired 'that Edward Spencer [*sic*] for his faulte, may be dewly tried and punished'. The *Vewe* was not licensed for publication in 1598. Spenser's voice never quite chimed harmoniously with official government policy. Throughout his career he shows a strong affection for the radical Protestant policies of the Earl of Leicester, who was in favour of a strong (and expensive) anti-Spanish policy in the Low Countries, and was consistently the patron of those who wished to see continuing reforms of the Protestant church at home. Even Spenser's later works – and particularly Book V of *The Faerie Queene*, which was printed in 1596 – hark back to this ideal, despite the death of Leicester in 1588. The fact that the Earl of Essex took responsibility for Spenser's funeral again suggests his links with the reforming faction at court. After the deaths of Leicester and Sidney, Essex became the chief source of patronage for poets whose Protestantism led them to press for continuing reform of the Church at home and an actively anti-Catholic policy abroad. Indeed, the chief quality that emerges from Spenser's life might be called – although it is a slightly odd use of the word – 'edginess'. He was a master at sitting on cultural boundaries: he was a poor scholar who reached the edges of court life; he praised the Queen, whilst never quite aligning himself with the policies which she wished to pursue. He was a poet who sat uneasily on the boundary between civilization and barbarism in Ireland. His poems, as we shall see, exploit this liminal position.

2

A Renaissance Poet

There were two extreme types of literary career in Elizabethan England. The first was that of the gentleman amateur, who would write poems or prose fiction for private circulation in manuscript form, and who would jealously strive to make it look as though any appearance of those works in print was not their responsibility. The most powerful example of this type of writer was Sir Philip Sidney, none of whose literary writings appeared in print during his lifetime. Sir Walter Ralegh, whom Spenser met in Ireland, also went to great lengths to avoid what has been called 'the stigma of print'. Extant copies of the popular anthology *England's Helicon* have slips labelled 'Ignoto' pasted over Ralegh's initials, which were presumably inserted by a nervous printer prompted by an irate author. George Puttenham remarked that 'I know very many notable Gentlemen in the Court that have written commendably, and suppressed it agayne, or els suffred it to be publisht without their owne names to it: as if it were a discredit for a Gentleman to seeme learned, and to show him selfe amorous of any good Art'.[1] At the other end of the literary spectrum were professional writers, who were often poor scholars from grammar schools, who went to university as sizars, and who then sought to scavenge a living in London from the press or from the stage. Christopher Marlowe and Thomas Nashe were the most famous examples of writers of this type, but for each of them there were a score of less talented, and less successful, hacks who found it hard to eat and harder to define their role in society. Robert Greene, for example, struggled to earn a living from pamphlets and plays, before dying in poverty and repentance in 1592. Midway along this scale were 'professional' writers who managed to win the patronage of noble men or women, or of the Queen herself. George Gascoigne composed entertainments for the Earl of

11

Leicester in 1575, and Ben Jonson, a pupil of William Camden at Westminster school, was later to become the well-rewarded writer of court masques for James I. The position of these writers was economically and socially delicate: they needed to print in order to become known, and they needed to dedicate their works to well-known figures in order to be rewarded for them. But publication brought with it the risk of blending into the mass of professional writers, and, perhaps too, of vulgarizing the reputation of one's patron. One way of negotiating these difficulties was to publish anonymously, with broad clues to one's identity, or to make it look as though one's works had been pirated by an unscrupulous printer. This would retain the cachet of privately circulated manuscript poetry, whilst gaining the publicity of print.

Spenser's first collection of verse was *The Shepheardes Calender*, published anonymously, and tentatively dedicated to Sir Philip Sidney in 1579. The book is elaborately crafted in order to create maximum impact and mystery, and to cut across the literary expectations of its audience. Its title is drawn from a popular handbook called *The Kalender of Shepherds*, which was first translated from French in 1503. This was a rustic almanac cum medicine cabinet cum prayerbook of Catholic leanings, which was reprinted so frequently that copies of it must have sat next to Bibles in houses and hovels throughout the land. Woodcuts ensured that its appeal would not be limited to the literate. Spenser's volume is designed to have the popular appeal of its model. Each of his eclogues is accompanied by a woodcut, some of which might remind the illiterate of a popular book, others of which might recall schoolroom editions of Virgil. The black letter type in which the poems are set would have looked decidedly old fashioned in 1579. A potential buyer, flipping through a copy, would find recurrent references to Colin Clout, who was a satirical and popular persona adopted by the early sixteenth-century poet John Skelton. The physical form of the book is nourished by the early stages of the English Reformation, and the whole work is designed to seem embedded in the popular energies of the nation. The volume is, however, also designed to exhibit the grandeur of a scholarly edition of a classical text. Each eclogue is preceded by an 'argument', or summary, and is followed by a learned, sometimes comically learned, set of notes by 'EK'. A would-be purchaser browsing over the stalls of Hugh Singleton, its printer, in 1579

12

would have been puzzled and excited by *The Shepheardes Calender*: here was a book which was modelled on the humblest kind of semi-literate chapbook, but which looked completely new in the grandeur with which it presented the work of an anonymous vernacular poet. It was an edgy work, one which straddled the boundaries between élite and popular forms of publication.[2]

The Shepheardes Calender also has the faint flavour of political opposition which so often emanates from Spenser's works. Its publisher was Hugh Singleton, who, five months before, had nearly had one of his hands chopped off for publishing *The Discoverie of a Gaping Gulf . . .* by the militant puritan John Stubbes. *The Gaping Gulf* was an attack on the Queen's flirtation with the Catholic Duc d'Alençon, which, had it developed into a marriage, might have returned the English Church to Roman Catholicism. Spenser's 'November' eclogue, with its lament for an unidentified princess called Dido (whose identity, EK nervously protests, 'is unknowen and closely buried in the Authors conceipt' (p.196)) has been seen as a representation of the nation's mourning for a queen who was in danger of dying to the faith (in Virgil's *Aeneid* Dido is also called 'Elissa' – not quite, but almost, Eliza). *The Shepheardes Calender* also repeatedly praises a shepherd called Algrind, whose purity is presented as a model for all pastors. Algrind is a transparent representation of Archbishop Grindal, who had been suspended from his duties as Archbishop of Canterbury in 1577 for his refusal to suppress lay preaching in his diocese. He had also written to the Queen protesting that royal influence on the Church and on lay piety had its limits. Grindal was a model for all those who wished that the Queen's conservative ecclesiastical policies would soften; and this popular religious hero, at odds with the will of the court, is the hero of the *Calender*'s ecclesiastical eclogues. For all its scent of opposition, and perhaps partly because of it, *The Shepheardes Calender* was the most popular of Spenser's works. It went through five editions in his lifetime, and rapidly inspired admiring and, occasionally, envious comment. It was *the* literary event of the 1570s.

The excitement is hard to recapture now. *The Shepheardes Calender* is partly designed to signal the emergence of a new poet, who, like Virgil before him, uses the sophisticatedly humble form of pastoral to initiate his career. The *Calender* contains many pre-echoes of Spenser's later style. Cuddie in 'September' promises to sing of 'fierce warres', as Spenser himself was to promise in the proem to *The Faerie Queene* that 'Fierce warres and faithful loues will moralize my song'. Hobbinol in 'June' recalls a song 'Whose Echo made the neyghbour groves to ring' (l. 52), and which joyously pre-echoes the varied chorus of Spenser's own *Epithalamion*, 'The woods shall to me answer and my Eccho ring'. But the bulk of *The Shepheardes Calender* is humbler fare, which, rather than pointing to the future, now has the musty flavour of second-hand bookshops. A modern reader will encounter shepherdly archaisms and dialect words throughout the volume. Sometimes, as in the start of 'Aprill', one is plunged straight into Middle English: 'what garres thee greete?', asks Thenot, and EK's gloss is as necessary now as it was to his first readers: what 'causeth thee weepe and complain'. Why write a poem which needed glossing even on its first publication? Spenser was partly imitating the theories of the French poet Du Bellay, whose *Défense et illustration de la langue Française* (1549) argues that the vernacular should be augmented by antique tongues and new coinages. Spenser was, that is, *innovating* by using old words. And many of the words which appear to be antiquated in *The Shepheardes Calender* are in fact words which Spenser introduced into the printed, literate language of his day. The *Oxford English Dictionary* attributes to Spenser the first usages of 'bellibone' (beautiful lady), 'wimble' (thought to be a northern dialect word for 'nimble'), and 'swink' (to work). Spenser can make powerful poetic use of the faintly antiqued resonances of these words. He writes in 'July' of hay which is 'frowie' ('musty'). A word which is itself mustily agricultural is used with brilliant precision to describe old hay. The word is not actually an archaism, but a word which Spenser brought into the language: like hay, its apparent oldness is potentially living and new. There are some howlers in Spenser's antiquey language: he invents the false archaic noun 'derring-do' (heroic deeds) from the Chaucerian verb 'derring-don' ('daring to do'); he also mistakenly thought that Chaucer's phrase 'The tigre yond in Inde' ('the tiger a long way away in India') meant 'the fierce tiger in India', and so can use 'yond' to mean 'ferocious'. These examples give some substance to Ben Jonson's accusation that 'Spenser, in Affecting the ancients, writ no Language';[3] but the overwhelming impact of *The Shepheardes Calender* is of amazing verbal innovation, in which even mistakes renovate the language, and extend its official sphere into new ranges of dialect. As EK's introduction says, the *Calender* is a work of renewal: 'he hath laboured to restore, as to theyr rightfull heritage such good and naturall English words, as have been long time out of use and almost cleare disherited' (p.16). Richard Mulcaster, Spenser's schoolmaster, had used a similarly political vocabulary when he described the expansion of English by the 'enfranchisement' of foreign words.[4] EK's suggestion that Spenser's language marks a liberation for native English words is worth taking seriously. A decade after the publication of *The Shepheardes Calender*, George Puttenham's *Arte of English Poesie* sought to close down the social inclusiveness of the *Calender's* vocabulary by insisting that would-be poets 'shall therefore take the usuall speach of the Court, and that of London and the shires lying about London within lx. miles and not much above'.[5] The *Calender* has no such exclusivity: this work by a successful poor scholar welcomes northern and Kentish forms into the language.

The most obvious thing to say about *The Shepheardes Calender* is that it is a calendar. It encompasses the whole year, from the deep-frozen buds of January, through the fitful warmth of March, the showers and flowers of April, into summer, and out into a withering September, a deadly November, and chill December. At every stage of the process the collection is aware that each stage *is* only a stage in a process. A welter of internal correspondences and recurrent images glance through the volume: tears are like frozen icicles in 'Januarye', by 'Aprill' they fall, promising fertility, into furrows. In 'June' they flow like overabundant sap from the leaves of trees; in 'November' they drop in unrelieved mourning; and finally in 'December' they dewily preserve the withered flowers of Colin Clout. 'Buds' are wasted with wailing in 'Januarye', are 'bloosming' (both blossoming and blooming) in 'Maye', and have turned into 'buddes of Poetrie', freeze-dried vitality, by 'October'. These running images invite a reader to recall, and to flip back to, earlier occurrences of them in order to build up an extended, seasonally adjusted, view of the year and its variety. A bud is both a frightened thing, securely enclosing itself against winter frosts, and a thrusting sign of spring. A tear can be icily isolating, or it can mark a sociable and reviving sorrow for another person. *The Shepheardes Calender*, that is, uses

15

its extended structure to build deep patterns of association, aimed to persuade that sorrow and joy, cold and life, are not antitheses but aspects of a continuing process. The governing rhetorical trope of the volume is oxymoron, a phrase which apparently contradicts itself. *The Shepheardes Calender* offers vital images of death, moments of chill which promise warmth – and presents itself as offering new oldness. There is no better evocation in English of what it feels like to live through a year, and to half-remember in January that dry twigs will eventually burgeon.

The *Calender* aims to create a coincidence of opposing moods. Its speakers are often grouped in opposing pairs, and seldom agree with each other. In 'August', for instance, Perigot has a singing-contest with Willye; while Perigot sings of his wounding by love's arrow, Willye answers him in incongruously jolly vein: 'There it rankleth more and more', laments Perigot, 'Hey ho the arrowe', chirrups Willye in reply. Moods interlace with one another, as the chilly old Thenot counters the youthful Cuddie in 'Februarie', but they never entirely overlap. The *Calender* is multi-perspectived art: what seems vital and optimistic in one character is at the same moment a source of melancholy for another. In 'Maye' Piers tells the Aesopian fable of a kid who is devoured by a wolf. The kid has a thrusting energy which suits the energy of the month:

> His Vellet head began to shoote out,
> And his wreathed hornes gan newly sprout,
> The blossomes of lust to bud did beginne,
> And spring forth ranckly under his chinne.

(ll. 185–8)

The verbs 'shoote', 'sprout', 'bud', and 'spring' link the life of the lamb with the vegetative energies of May. But for the kid's mother, signs of life prompt memories of sadness.

> A thrilling throbbe from her hart did aryse,
> And interrupted all her other speache,
> With some old sorowe, that made a newe breache:
> Seemed shee sawe in the younglings face
> The old lineaments of his fathers grace.

(ll. 208–12)

'Thrilling' is one of Spenser's favourite words. He often uses it to evoke a sudden pang of emotion, the violent irruption of an unexpected voice into silence, or the sudden stab of Cupid's arrow. Here it catches the sharp anguish of being reminded of an old sorrow by something new and fresh. Newness and life are celebrated in the *Calender*, but are tied in with sadness: rebirth of a new generation depends upon the death of the old. William Ponsonby, the printer of *Complaints*, reports that Spenser paraphrased Ecclesiastes. Whether or not he did so, the mingling of life and death, and the dependency of the one on the other, which Ecclesiastes so mournfully explores, is the founding principle of much of Spenser's most painfully fresh writing. EK's Epistle notes that *The Shepheardes Calender* applies 'an olde name to a new worke' (p.19). That line 'With some old sorowe, that made a newe breache' could stand as an epigraph for the whole: old pain makes new wounds; the new painfully recalls the old.

The central figure in *The Shepheardes Calender* is the poet Colin Clout, whom Spenser adopted as his own persona throughout his literary career. He is not a successful shepherd: when we meet him in 'Januarye' his sheep are starving, and he is bewailing the hardheartedness of his mistress Rosalind. When we leave him in 'December' he is on the brink of death. His poems include only one moment of joyous control, and only one moment when poet and court seem to be identified, when he sings of Eliza, Queene of Shepheardes, in 'Aprill':

> See, where she sits upon the grassie greene,
>   (O seemely sight)
> Yclad in Scarlot like a mayden Queene,
>   And Ermines white.
> Upon her head a Cremosin coronet,
> With Damaske roses and Dafadillies set.
>
> (ll. 55–60)

At this moment Colin seems almost himself to be making the Queen, directing our gaze towards her, and shaping her garments to reflect the image of her which he wishes to convey. It is the first of many Spenserian moments of framed vision (which abound in *The Faerie Queene*), when the poet fashions a pageant with a woman at its centre. But this moment of poetic centrality is evanescent: Colin is not present in 'Aprill' to sing his poem (his friend Hobbinol sings it for him), since he has devoted his life to the solitary business of bewailing his unsuccessful love. His role

17

as a court poet is placed in the past. He has become a poet whose idiom is lament, who listens to the melancholy echoes of his own voice from the woods and rocks through which he wanders. He complains in 'June', sings a plaintive sestina (a stanzaic poem in which each of the six rhyming words is repeated at the end of a different line in each stanza) in 'August', and returns in 'November' to bemoan the death of Dido. In 'December' he describes how his life dwindles towards a wintry isolation, cut off from the court, and insulated from the sources of life. Moralizing critics have been hard on Colin, and have argued that he is a representative of a self-obsessed, inward-looking poetry which was anathema to Spenser. But throughout his career Spenser pressed for a virtual equivalence between the sources of poetry and a sense of loss. Indeed perhaps the chief goal of his shorter works is to create a poetic which attaches significance to poets who lack either patronage or an active role in court. The argument to 'October' states that 'In Cuddie is set out the perfecte paterne of a Poete, which finding no maintenaunce of his state and studies, complayneth of the comtempte of Poetrie, and the causes thereof' (p.170). Cuddie himself is obsessed by the loss of past patrons ('But ah *Mecœnas* is yclad in claye, | And great *Augustus* long ygoe is dead' (ll. 61–2)) in a way that suggests he is not quite 'the perfecte paterne of a Poete'. But he does share a sense of loss with the *Calender*'s plaintive central persona, Colin Clout. Colin Clout's melancholy, however, is seldom without a consoling power. His laments, like the whole *Calender*, mingle a sense of loss with joyful renewal. When Colin laments the death of the ideal English poet, Chaucer, his plaintful elegy is aware that the death of a predecessor can generate life for the poets who follow him:

> Nowe dead he is, and lyeth wrapt in lead,
> (O why should death on hym such outrage showe?)
> And all hys passing skil with him is fledde,
> The fame whereof doth dayly greater growe.
> But if on me some little drops would flowe,
> Of that the spring was in his learned hedde,
> I soone would learne these woods, to wayle my woe,
> And teache the trees their trickling teares to shedde.
>
> ('June', ll. 89–96)

At first this seems simply glum. But the whole stanza has just the paradoxical combination of gloom and vitality which runs

18

through *The Shepheardes Calender* as a whole. Chaucer's fame still grows, along with the vegetative life of June, and his liquid influence (springs in the *Calender* are as life-giving as the season with which they share their name) nourishes Colin's mournful song. Learning from the dead how to lament the dead is how poetry continues to grow. *The Shepheardes Calender* is often seen as a work which straddles the boundary between 'medieval' and 'Renaissance'. Its interest in the power and immortality of verse, and its determined construction of a powerful persona for Colin Clout, have been seen as its most distinctively 'Renaissance' aspects, since, it is often thought, the key element in Renaissance attitudes to poetry is a sense of the power and dignity of the poet. Precedent for all these things can be found in Chaucer and his successors, however.[6] Rather, what makes the collection distinctively the work of a Renaissance poet is the feature which seems at first to be its most medieval element: its conscious oldness, and its conscious identification of the power of a modern poet with his capacity to complain about the loss of the past. *The Shepheardes Calender* makes its readers aware that there is a space between the present and a literary past, and that a poet is growing anew from his efforts to bridge that gap. The word 'Renaissance', of course, is not used in English before the nineteenth century, and certainly would not have been used by Spenser himself. But it is an appropriate term to describe the period between Petrarch and Milton, since poetry in that period is preoccupied with a desire to revive dead classical learning. This desire permeates the literary criticism of the period, which frequently uses metaphors of disinterring, of raising the dead to life, and of biological reproduction to describe how new poets grow from old. *The Shepheardes Calender* is a deliberate attempt to mark a poetic rebirth in England; but that rebirth comes, oddly, from the death of the old. Death and life feed each other reciprocally.

The Shepheardes Calender probably created expectations in its original audience that its accomplished but anonymous author would go on to attempt greater things. Its chief generic model is Virgil's *Eclogues*, which Virgil followed by his *Georgics* (a didactic poem about farming) and his epic, the *Aeneid*. An early reader of the *Calender* might have expected that its author might carry on with a similar literary career. These expectations were in part fulfilled by the publication in 1590 of the first three books of

Spenser's allegorical epic, *The Faerie Queene* (which will be discussed in later chapters). But in 1591 Spenser's career might have seemed to take an odd side-step with the publication of a volume of shorter poems, called *Complaints: Containing sundrie small Poemes of the Worlds Vanitie*. This volume is presented by its printer, William Ponsonby, as a collection which he had 'gathered togeather' from poems which were previously 'disperst abroad in sundrie hands' (p. 223), but it is very likely that Spenser, who was probably in London as the volume went to press, had a part in its construction, and designed it to fill out the lines of his persona, already sketched in *The Shepheardes Calender*, as a plaintful poet. It contains an odd mixture of some very early poems (the 'Visions of Bellay' are revised versions of poems which appeared in the *Theatre for Worldlings* of 1569, and the 'Visions of Petrarch' are described as 'formerly translated') and some which, such as 'Mother Hubberd', seem to have been revised quite recently to reflect topical concerns. The collection rings the changes on the theme of complaint, ranging from universal misery to specifically directed satirical attacks. Through the 'Teares of the Muses', which laments the neglect of the arts, to the 'Ruines of Time', in which the ancient Romano-British town of Verulamium laments the fall of herself, that of Rome, and the imminent collapse of the universe, Spenser explores cosmic and universal misery. In the sharply satirical 'Mother Hubberds Tale' he complains against the court, and, obliquely, Lord Burghley. The mood of the volume, with the exception of the lightly woven tale of the butterfly, 'Muiopotmos', is gloomy. Sidney is dead, Leicester is dead. Walsingham is dead. The Muses are neglected. Rome and Verulamium have decayed into dust. 'O trustlesse state of miserable men' ('Ruines of Time', l. 197) might serve as an epigraph to the whole volume, of which the strongest moments are of bludgeoning, almost bathetic gloom: 'He dyde, and after him his brother dyde' ('Ruines of Time', l. 239). Its melancholy tone – surpassed only in Spenser's output by the elegy *Daphnaïda* – lacks the counterpoising optimism which is generated by the calendrical structure of *The Shepheardes Calender*: misery is not seen in the context of a transient season, but is seen as misery. And universalized.

The *Complaints* volume is designed to build on the vision of the poet presented in *The Shepheardes Calender* as a person who makes writing out of loss and who makes something new by emphasizing the pastness of the past. It also, though, contains some elements which indicate that Spenser had not completely set aside the Virgilian trajectory for his career which is implicit in *The Shepheardes Calender*. The volume includes 'Virgils Gnat', which translates a Latin poem, widely believed in the Renaissance to have been by Virgil, about a gnat which saves a sleeping shepherd from a snake by biting him awake, and who is then killed for his pains. The poem hints that this is an allegory of the way that powerful people ignore the admonitions of humble poets. The presence of 'Virgils Gnat' is important for understanding the role played by *Complaints* in Spenser's career: it suggests that there is Virgilian precedent for allegorical verse, and that there is Virgilian precedent too for plaintful writing about the mistreatment of poets whose apparently marginal voices can offer good counsel to the powerful. Where the *Complaints* volume rises above misery – and it does not often do so – it suggests that there is a positive power to complaining, that neglected poets have matters of state import to utter, and that poets who lament the loss of the past can revive that past through lament. Complaint is not a form which is invented by Spenser – it plays a significant role in Chaucer's output, and complaints from Chaucer's longer works were frequently anthologized in manuscript miscellanies – but it can prompt him to explore what it is to be a Renaissance poet, attempting to catch from a distance and to re-echo the vanishing voices of the past. 'The Ruines of Rome: by Bellay' provides some magnificently fragile visions of what it is to be a poet preoccupied with the revival of dead verse, who listens for the shrill voices of the past re-echoing from the decayed monuments of Rome. The first sonnet in the sequence begins:

> Ye heavenly spirites, whose ashie cinders lie
> Under deep ruines, with huge walls opprest,
> But not your praise, the which shall never die
> Through your faire verses, ne in ashes rest;
>   If so be shrilling voyce of wight alive
> May reach from hence to depth of darkest hell,
> Then let those deep Abysses open rive,
> That ye may understand my shreiking yell.

(ll. 1–8)

The substance of this sonnet is all in Du Bellay's French original, but Spenser brings to it a sharpness of sound, and a piercing loneliness. His voice thrills out of a landscape sketched of ruins and darkness, desperate to communicate with the dead, and to hear their voices. The immortality promised by fame and poetic revival is enclosed within an atmosphere of mortality, creating a blend of fragility and aspiration to renew which is pure Spenser. The Envoy to the 'Ruines of Rome' attributes the power of rebirth to Du Bellay, who managed 'Olde *Rome* out of her ashes to revive, | And give a second life to dead decayes' (ll. 453–4). Whilst he praises Du Bellay for reviving the dead, Spenser himself creates a new and living vocabulary of death. *OED* does not cite a plural use of 'decays' to mean 'ruins, debris' before 1615, although this must be the sense in which Spenser uses the word here. The *Complaints* volume uses the very new verbal form of 'ruin', and repeatedly uses the verb 'rehearse' on the boundary between 'recite a poem' and 're-entomb'. And this double sense captures the spirit of the plaintful side of Spenser: after death poetry still lives on, rehearsing, reintombing, and reviving at once its ancient woes. The *Complaints* offer new words for the loss of the past, and seek to create new poems from its echoes.

For the majority of the 1590s Spenser was in Ireland, and his strongest memories of England were of an era which had passed. He was in both a physical and a historical sense an exile: he was geographically removed from court; and that court no longer contained the Protestant noblemen – Sidney, Leicester, and Walsingham – who had afforded him patronage, or the hope of it, in the 1570s and 1580s. This put him in a position of isolation from his ideals, his home land, his own past – and put pressure on him to fashion a set of poetic concerns which might enable him to gain strength from his unhappy situation. The fashioning of the *Complaints* may well have owed something to these circumstances; but *Colin Clouts Come Home Againe*, which appeared in 1595, presents the fullest expression of Spenser's sense of dislocation. Colin relates to an audience of Irish shepherds how he exchanged verses with the Shepherd of the Ocean, Spenser's fellow planter in Ireland, Sir Walter Ralegh. This section locates 'home' firmly in Ireland, as Colin sings of the marriage of two Irish rivers, and becomes a poet of the Irish landscape. The early sections of the poem also link the sources of poetry with complaint, as the Shepherd of the Ocean sings of his neglect by Cynthia. The two

22

shepherds then go to court, at which point the poem mingles praises of courtly ladies, court poets, and the person of Cynthia with savage attacks on the failures of courtiers to favour learning or to do more than corruptly love. It ends with praise of love, and in particular of Colin's love Rosalind. It is an extraordinary poem, which suggests how strongly Spenser in this period was attempting to find a way of writing which would enable strength to come from exile. Exile in Ireland becomes a stable location from which to judge and condemn the lack of patronage at court; and the corruptions of court provide an excuse for turning to compose hymns of love, and for demanding that corrupt courtly lovers themselves 'Exuls out of his [love's] court be thrust' (l. 894). The volume in which the poem appears is filled out with Spenser's 'Astrophel', a pastoral lament for Sir Philip Sidney, and with other elegies on Sidney by, among others, Spenser's chief friend in Ireland, Lodovic Bryskett. Sidney had been dead for nearly ten years by the time the volume appeared, and this time lag between death and lament is significant. The *Colin Clout* volume is not just retrospective; it is polemically retrospective. The collection is designed to suggest that there is a community of New English poets in Ireland who are exiles in mourning for a lost Protestant past, and who draw their poetic energies from the lost world of the 1580s. It is a volume which is trying to make imaginative strength out of not being at the centre of English life.

Spenser's other poems of the mid-1590s mark a distinct movement away from court, and root themselves in his own Irish circumstances. His *Amoretti and Epithalamion* of 1595 are concerned with his courtship of Elizabeth Boyle, and fulfil the promise of Colin Clout to sing less of court and more of love. The sonnet sequence turns away from the public realm of *The Faerie Queene* towards more private subjects. In Sonnet 33, addressed to his friend Lodovic Bryskett, Spenser apologizes for his vagrancy from the task of finishing *The Faerie Queene*; but it is clear from the style of the poems in the volume that the poet is enjoying the opportunity to forget about Queen and court. The *Epithalamion*, a poem on Spenser's own marriage, is one of his best-known and most harmoniously universal poems: the number of long lines in it (365) reflects the number of days in the year, and night comes after sixteen and a quarter stanzas, reflecting the number of hours of daylight on the actual day (11 June) of Spenser's marriage. It is a poem which subliminally asserts its universal status, whilst also being geared to the peculiar life and concerns of its poet. It grows from a hollow chorus of Spenser's characteristically plaintful landscape ('So I unto my selfe alone will sing, I The woods shall to me answer and my Eccho ring' (ll. 17–18)) into a vision of a social and religious gathering at the poet's marriage. The poem is almost oppressively controlled by its maker, as though at this stage in his career Spenser is intent upon fashioning and inhabiting his own perfect world. The price of this is paid by the bride: Elizabeth Boyle is entirely contained within Spenser's ordered and ordering verse:

> And let the ground whereas her foot shall tread,
> For feare the stones her tender foot should wrong,
> Be strewed with fragrant flowers all along.

(ll. 48–50)

Biographical legend has it that Elizabeth Boyle escaped from the Irish rebels who destroyed Kilcolman in 1598 via its underground passages. The start of her married life also has its claustrophobic side. The tone of the *Epithalamion* is that of a nervy bridegroom ordering the show, or of a poet intent upon making a perfect structure for his love. But Elizabeth is scarcely there at all. The poem contains (on a rough count) 115 imperative verbs in 430 lines. Although many of these are gentle 'let's', the cumulative effect is of dominating command. The actual moment of marriage passes with only a blush from the lady, for which the poet – albeit gently – rebukes her ('Why blush ye love to give to me your hand, I The pledge of all our band' (ll. 238–9)). Spenser is a poet who wishes to be a 'maker' in the very strong sense that the word had in the sixteenth century, which is aware of analogies with the divine maker of the universe. But in the *Epithalamion* he is also aware of the fragility of his own poetic structure, and of the fact that it exists against a backdrop of time over which he has no control. Its most moving lines are an address to Phoebus, the sun:

> But let this day let this one day be myne,
> Let all the rest be thine.

(ll. 125–6)

This is the only point in the poem when the word 'let' occurs twice in the same line, and marks a desperate appeal. It indicates

24

one of the strongest features of Spenser's shorter verse. For all his efforts to control the world of his poems, he is aware that a poetic maker is part of a larger world, a world which will not go the faster, or the slower, for his driving.

In the *Prothalamion*, a poem celebrating the betrothals of Elizabeth and Katherine Somerset, and the last of Spenser's poems to be printed in his lifetime (1596), the poet's voice begins, as is its wont, plaintively alone and on the edge of court life: 'Through discontent of my long fruitlesse stay I In Princes Court' (ll. 6–7). But it weaves itself intimately into the natural world with the magical fluency of its repeated refrain 'Sweete *Themmes* runne softly, till I end my Song', and grows to an echoing harmony, joining the poet's lone voice to those of the nymphs who attend the ceremony and to the mute signs of pleasure given by the river Lea. The *Prothalamion*, however, is well aware that a Renaissance poet inhabits a larger world. The Thames will, of course, flow softly on before, during, and after Spenser's plaintful song, and its presence murmuring in the background places the solitary poet against a wider framework, softening the edge of his plaintive song. The poem closes, oddly for a spousal verse, with a vision of the Earl of Essex, who, Spenser predicts, will revive the spirit of the Earl of Leicester, and free the country from 'forraine harmes' (l. 156), 'Which some brave muse may sing I To ages following' (ll. 159–60). This vision of Essex marks the *Prothalamion* as at once a bid for patronage from this Protestant nobleman and an effort to revive the spirit of the dead Earl of Leicester. Within three years of the poem's publication, however, Spenser was dead, and Essex's chief contribution to the poet's welfare was to pay for his burial. Two years later Essex himself was executed, having raised a failed palace *coup* against his Queen. The beseeching voice of the *Prothalamion* fades into the background of history, of forces which the poet cannot shape. At the end of *The Shepheardes Calender* Colin Clout is not triumphantly in control of his world, but is crawling towards death, shaped by, rather than shaping, the seasons of the year; and in the *Epithalamion* the poet cannot, for all his beseeching, stop the sinking of the sun. Part of Spenser's imagination is totalizing: it seeks to control the elements and mimic the universal process of life and time. But an equal and opposite side of his imagination is aware that he is a mortal poet – one who is subject to time, to change, and to the unpredictable motions of patronage and royal favour. This double-aspected vision can produce a poetry which is astoundingly moving: a lone voice plains against a backdrop of natural and political processes, a backdrop which at once sustains and erodes the poet's vision. These two aspects of Spenser's art come together in a brilliantly volatile manner in what is by far his greatest poem, *The Faerie Queene*.

3

Dynastic Epic

The Faerie Queene is an extraordinarily difficult poem to grasp. By this I do not mean only that it is a difficult book to pick up -- though the effort of enclosing the spine of some editions of the poem would stretch the largest of hands. It is a work of which the chief delight is elusiveness. It digresses; it continually changes tone and tack; and it never gets to the point (the vision of Gloriana in all her glory) which it sets as its chief goal. The poem slips through one's fingers as one reads. The smooth flow of the Spenserian stanza creates a beguilingly homogeneous surface, in which an apparently heroic knight could turn out to be a disguised magician, or a lady crying for pity could turn out to be a figure of the Antichrist. Dwarfs, dragons, hermits, witches, women made of snow, forest-dwelling virgins, all drift smoothly by, captured in the flow of Spenser's language, sealed in the music of his unique nine-line stanzas. The 'Spenserian stanza', as it came to be known, rhyming ababbcbcc, and ending with a twelve-syllable line, or alexandrine, invites repose: the rhymes interlock and lace back into each other, and the final line draws its slow length along, inviting readerly delay. The form of the poem fights a continual benevolent war with its content. The knights who dominate the action are tasked with pursuing villains, liberating nations, or reuniting lovers. Their efforts to move purposively onwards requires them to struggle against the reflective flow of Spenser's verse, which ebbs backwards endlessly.

The poem, huge, digressive, as big, as incompletable, and as complex as the business of living, was always slightly running away from its author. Appended to its first edition in 1590 (which included the first three books) was a Letter to Ralegh, which states that all the adventures related in the planned twelve books of the poem would ultimately come to rest at the annual feast of

Gloriana. The parts of the poem which were printed – six books and two Cantos of Mutabilitie – never fulfil this grand design, and offer no more than a glimpse of Gloriana the Faerie Queene. She is only described in a dream, which, as Arthur describes it, leaves its dreamer with no more than a flavour of delight when he awakes ('But whether dreames delude, or true it were, I Was neuer hart so rauisht with delight' (I. ix. 14)). The poem at its best convinces its readers both that they are going somewhere, and that that somewhere may be, well, not quite real nor ever quite reachable. The Letter to Ralegh also gives very inaccurate paraphrases of the plots of the books which follow it, wrong-footing its readers from their very first point of contact with the work. The architecture of *The Faerie Queene*, its narrative line and structure, its significance and form, repeatedly defeats its readers, but they should be reassured that it also often proved too much for its author. Several times Spenser gets his own poem wrong: the arguments to several cantos mistake the names of characters or the description of actions which follow, and on a couple of occasions Spenser seems to forget which of his multiple knights is where. At the start of Book III he fails to remember that Guyon should have already left the castle of Alma, and goes on to confuse Guyon with Redcrosse in III. ii. At VI. vi. 17 he writes Calidore when he means Calepine. In III. iv he makes Britomart wound Marinell, and thereby initiate the flight of Florimell which had already occurred three cantos before. The title of Book IV contains the oddest of these inconsistencies: it tells us that Book IV contains 'the Legend of Cambel and Telamond', and yet the hero of the book is called 'Triamond'. Many of these moments indicate simple mechanical errors at the late stages of revision; others seem teasingly artful – it is, after all, entirely appropriate that an unfinished poem should fail to contain a character called 'Telamond', whose name suggests the end or perfecting (*telos*) of the world. But they also point to a much wider feature of *The Faerie Queene*: Spenser could not write exactly the poem he wished to write, because he was subject to forces which he could not quite control. All writers are subject to the frailties of circumstance; but Spenser uses and dramatizes the forces which push his poem into odd shapes with an artfulness unsurpassed by any other writer. His political circumstances, and the traditions of writing which he inherited and which he tried to transform, all make his poem, with his own half-collusion, spin away from its proposed goals. Despite his wish to be a shaping artist, Colin Clout becomes a poet in the *December* eclogue who passively compares his life with the passing of the year. In *The Faerie Queene* the forces which pull the poet off course are stronger and more deeply imbedded in the texture of the materials which he is using; but it has this much in common with his earlier poems: it slightly – perhaps heroically – fails to be the poem it sets itself to be. And it uses the pressures which bear down upon it to become one of the most endlessly elusive, teasingly ravishing poems in the language.

One of those pressures was the tradition of epic as it reached Spenser. This is a genre which is out of fashion these days, and which is generally reckoned to be demandingly long and hard. Epic poems, though, were originally just long poems which recorded the doings of heroes. The earliest Western epics were composed orally (that is, as the poet recited) by a bard who was skilled in a repertoire of variable phrases which he could adapt in new contexts to create a continuingly varied song. Homer was probably the greatest of these poets, who brought a repertoire of stories related by earlier, lost, heroic poets into an unusually well-formed shape. His tales were already of the past (he, or maybe the group of people whom we call Homer, probably lived in the eighth century BC, and wrote about mythical events which had their roots in actions which probably occurred in the thirteenth century BC). An element of wonder at the amazing feats of his heroes, and a sense that men nowadays cannot hope to emulate their actions, is part of the epic style he established. Spenser probably read some Homer at school, but the influence of the *Iliad* and the *Odyssey* on *The Faerie Queene* is slight. Moments such as Guyon's heroic voyage to the Bowre of Blisse at the end of Book II have a Homeric flavour: where Homer's Odysseus avoids the rocks inhabited by Scylla and the whirlpool of Charybdis, Guyon, the modern allegorical hero, has to shun the 'Rocke of Reproch' and the 'Whirlepool of decay'. When he alludes to or imitates Homer, Spenser usually thinks first of the generations of allegorical commentary which had grown up around the poems, rather than the works themselves.

A greater influence on *The Faerie Queene* is Virgil's epic, the *Aeneid*. Virgil's earliest commentator, Servius, said that Virgil's intention in writing the poem was to imitate Homer and to praise his emperor Augustus through praising his parents. This is naturally not the whole story, but it usefully points the chief difference between Virgil and Homer. Virgil aimed to tell a laudatory history of the early stages of his own country. He also aimed, in the process, to create a new type of hero in his Aeneas, who is aware that his nation has a history, and is aware that problems lie in the way of realizing that history, and who is also, and above all, superior to his Homeric predecessors. A great feature of the *Aeneid* is the way it uses the repetitions necessitated by Homer's formulaic style artfully: Virgil repeats phrases in different contexts with an awareness of resonances between their different usages. Characters who die fighting against Aeneas (of whom there are many) are often described in phrases which deliberately recall those which are used to describe the deaths of those who fight for him. Empire and its enemies are disturbingly similar in the *Aeneid*, and these similarities extend to the hero himself. In the final book of the *Aeneid* Aeneas kills his enemy Turnus in a burst of rage, and the poem ends with a jolt as Turnus' spirit flees to the shades. The hero has to become like his irascible enemy in order to defeat him. By this unsettling action Aeneas enables his marriage to Turnus's fiancée, Lavinia, and thereby ensures the future unfolding of his dynasty.

Most editions of Virgil in the Renaissance included a thirteenth book, added to the *Aeneid* by the fifteenth-century poet Mapheus Vegius. In this book Aeneas is not left, as he is in Virgil's possibly incomplete, or possibly deliberately bitter, concluding episode, standing over a dead enemy, but, in a manner that is aware of the mildness appropriate to a Christian hero, he marries Lavinia. Vegius effectively turned the *Aeneid* into what has been called a 'dynastic epic.'[1] That is, he makes it into a poem which ends in a marriage, and the inception of a blood-line of heroes. This change to the nature of epic runs profoundly counter to the ethos of the Homeric poems, in which marriage is important as a force which sustains the household, but has little power as an emotional bond, or as a motive for heroic action. It was lovingly adopted, however, in fifteenth- and sixteenth-century Italy, where a generation of writers who were steeped in medieval chivalric romances, and aware too of classical traditions of epic, produced one of the greatest hybrid genres of the Renaissance: epic romance. Matteo Maria Boiardo (?1441–94) wrote a huge, digressively funny poem

called *Orlando innammorato* (Orlando Smitten with Love) in which
the chief joke is the title. Orlando is the French warrior hero of the
Chanson de Roland, who spends his life in heroically destructive
martial deeds. Boiardo makes him go mad with love, and creates
an unfinished, sprawling, stanzaic poem, partly about Orlando's
efforts to win the Saracen princess Angelica (which he never
succeeds in doing), and partly about the efforts of other characters
to marry (which they seldom manage to do). Giants and orcs
abound. Ludovico Ariosto (1474–1533) – the most exuberantly
brilliant writer of the Italian Renaissance – tried to complete
Boiardo's poem in *Orlando furioso* (Orlando the Mad). In Ariosto's
poem, which was the most popular narrative poem in Renaissance
Europe, Orlando is still desperately seeking Angelica, whom he
still fails to win. There is also a dynastic couple, Ruggiero and his
heroic lady Bradamante, who, after innumerable brushes with orcs,
wicked sorceresses, magic rings, and so forth, do actually succeed
in marrying each other. Their union founds the dynasty of the
D'Este family, who were Ariosto's patrons at the court of Ferrara.

There is an air of incompleteness, or indeed of incompletability
(if that is a word), to sixteenth-century epic romance. Although
Ariosto finished his poem, after his death were printed five further
cantos which do not quite tie in with the action of the poem as we
have it. He also revised the poem considerably in his lifetime.
Provisionality and improvisation are key features of the mode. The
game played by a story-teller such as Ariosto is to 'interlace' (that
is, to weave into each other) as many different tales as he can. So,
as one strand of his wonderfully over-woven text is reaching a
climax – as, say, a knight nearly gets his gauntlets on Angelica –
he will mischievously intrude, and remind us that another strand
of his story requires attention. The effect is deliberately hard to
follow, but it allows stories to comment on each other, and it
allows the author to remain always ungraspably one step ahead of
his audience. It also evokes a world in which human desire is
endlessly unfulfillable, and in which a dynastic history of fulfilled
love is ever more about to happen.

Ariosto's poem reached Spenser walled about with thick
allegorical commentaries which nervy editors, such as Simon
Fornari, added to damp down the more obviously excessive
exuberances and sexual lightnesses of *Orlando furioso*. Spenser
was also aware, although probably not when he started to write

The Faerie Queene in the early 1580s, of the more sober example of the *Gerusalemme liberata* (Jerusalem Liberated) of Torquato Tasso (1544–95). Tasso's theoretical writings (his *Discourses on the Heroic Poem*) worry about the marvellous events contained in, and the formal disunity of, earlier Italian romances, and argue that the epic poem should combine unity and plurality, like the world itself. His poem is chiefly interesting for its efforts, painful and forcible efforts, to control the sprawling and erotic energies of the romance mode, and to forge from them a unified work, with a single main action, along the lines of Virgil's *Aeneid*. It also has an explicitly Christian subject: the Christian forces labour to free Jerusalem from their irascible and blasphemous pagan adversaries. The poem as Spenser saw it contained many vestiges of the romance mode, in erotic episodes and pastoral digressions. Tasso subsequently refined many of these out of his poem to create the simply triumphalist and often simply dull *Gerusalemme conquistata* (Jerusalem Conquered). He also appended to the poem an allegory, which sees the actions of the heroes, as they strive to suppress their love of pagan ladies in order to concentrate on the liberation of the Holy City, as allegorically figuring the efforts of the reason to control the rebellious passions. There is an excellent translation of Tasso's poem by Edward Fairfax (1600), which is influenced by Spenser's style, and gives a strong impression of how Spenser would have perceived the work.

Epic romance in the late sixteenth century, then, was a form creatively at war with itself. It had its roots in a sparklingly light form, breeding digression on digression, driving itself towards fulfilment in marriage; but it grew to take on weightier matter – an aspiration towards severe moral significance and a corresponding economy of narrative line. The long and complicated debates in the sixteenth century about the form which a modern epic should take – about whether it should concentrate on martial, heroic actions, and have a ruthlessly unified structure, or be allowed to digress endlessly, as amorous heroes range around the world failing to find their loves – all fuel the alternately wandering and purposive structure of *The Faerie Queene*. No reader can fail to feel that sometimes Spenser is entranced by moments which delay his heroes' quests. To pause over a tapestry from which wanton eyes flash out provocatively, to cast a wistful glance at a bathing maiden, to wish to rush off and assist a pitiful but deceptive woman, these are all actions in which knights and readers seem to collaborate with the privy wishes of the author. Again and again arguments about the form of epic romance become internal structural debates within *The Faerie Queene*, between the desire to delay and digress, and the need to proceed purposively and significantly onwards. Books I and II are roughly linear, and roughly parallel, in plot and conception. That is, their heroes have a main goal – in Redcrosse's case it is killing the dragon, in Guyon's it is the conquest of Acrasia – which they achieve in the last two cantos of their respective books. Their adventures are studded with digressions, when they are dragged off course by seductive and deceptive women, or are lured into dark places by allegorical personifications such as Despaire or Mamon, but these episodes are signalled as secondary actions and subordinated to their main goal. In Book III, however, the balance of this linear structure is disrupted: the action becomes extremely digressive, and the plot complicatedly interlaced, in the manner of earlier sixteenth-century romance. Britomart apparently has no clear quest when we first encounter her. She just happens to unhorse Guyon in Canto i. Then Spenser inserts a flashback which relates her girlhood, and which belatedly reveals the motivation for her quest. Britomart is in search of an elusive love, Arthegall, whom she has seen only in a magic mirror, and whom she has learnt is to be her dynastic partner. The kinds of erotic digression which in Books I and II had almost always signalled a dangerous abandonment of the chief goal become in Book III something to be relished. The action can slow down to admit rambling interludes with the false knight Braggadocchio, or it can recoil into an unspecified past to dwell on the procreative energies of the Garden of Adonis. And it never arrives at the union of Britomart and Arthegall which it proposes as its ending.

We can be fairly sure that Spenser began to shape *The Faerie Queene* in the early 1580s, since Harvey makes some disapproving remarks about the 'Elvish Queene' in one of the *Letters*, and advises Spenser to concentrate on writing plays instead. It is very likely that at this stage Spenser was planning to write a dynastic romance modelled on *Orlando furioso*, and that Book III contains some of the earliest sections of the poem to have been composed. Most of his literary heroes at this time were European writers from the first decades of the sixteenth century, such as the French

poet Clement Marot (1496–1544), to whom there are many
allusions in *The Shepheardes Calender*, and Ariosto was the most
popular author in Europe. In 1580 it was still just possible that the
Queen would marry. As we have seen, her courtship by the
Catholic Duc d'Alençon in 1579 has an impact on *The Shepheardes
Calender*. So at that time, Spenser, who was in the employment of
the Earl of Leicester, could have planned a huge, digressive poem
which might have ended, majestically, with Gloriana's marriage
to a figure, Arthur, who represented the idealized history of
Protestant Britain, and who might, in certain lights, have had a
trick of the Earl to him. Writing this sort of poem rapidly became
impossible, even if it had ever been entirely feasible. As the
wrinkles began increasingly to win the battles with the rouge in
Queen Elizabeth's morning toilette, the likelihood of her marrying
lessened. Spenser's poem, as it grew through the 1580s, came to
exploit the irresolvability of the epic form as he received it: a
dynastic marriage had to recede endlessly into the future if he
was to dedicate the poem to Elizabeth. *The Faerie Queene* also uses
the wistfulness of the epic mode, its recurrent tendency to locate
the true moment of heroic civilization either in the past, as Homer
had done, or in the future, where in Virgil's *Aeneid* an imperial
destiny hides ever more about to be, to defer its unattainable
ending. The dynastic marriages which the poem repeatedly
promises never occur. The Rivers Thames and Medway marry in
Book IV, and their union enables Marinell finally to be united
with his love Florimell. Elsewhere in the poem characters seek
each other, and sometimes find each other; but they then part,
postponing the ideal union of male and female to the outer
reaches of our vision. At the end of Book I, Redcrosse is betrothed
to Una, and then returns to fight more battles for his Faerie
Queene. In Book IV Britomart and Arthegall meet, become
engaged, and then part. A dynastic epic for a maiden Queen is a
curious thing: virginity, the chief virtue of Spenser's Queen and
dedicatee, was antipathetic to the whole governing design of his
poem. And the great power of *The Faerie Queene* is that its
wistfulness, its teasingly idealizing spirit, is partly the product of
an effort to write such an impossible work.

The poem also attempts to be an epic about British history, and
wishes to weld the history of Britain and its rulers onto the
framework of classical epic. On the face of it the most obvious way

in which to do this would have been to make the heroes and heroines of *The Faerie Queene* the biological descendants of the chief characters of, say, Virgil's *Aeneid*. This would give to British history, and to Spenser's chief characters, the authority of classical precedent. It would also make Spenser's poem appear to be in a near-literal sense a rebirth of classical epic, since it would explore the heroic actions of the biological successors to Virgil's Aeneas. However, Spenser's awareness of the fact that his Queen's own family was at an end shapes every level of his writing. The goal of dynastic heroes is to marry and to breed, in order to continue the line of their parents, and this will to breed is burned deeply in the imagery of *The Faerie Queene*: Arthur, when we first meet him, has been searching for Gloriana for nine months, the period of human gestation; and the quest for glory is at one point compared to the process of biological reproduction:

> The noble hart, that harbours vertuous thought,
> And is with child of glorious great intent,
> Can neuer rest, vntill it forth haue brought
> Th'eternall brood of glorie excellent.

(I. v. 1)

The literal 'brood of glorie', however, never emerges to the light in the poem. *The Faerie Queene* is extremely uneasy about presenting unified, completed histories of successful dynasties which live on endlessly through reproduction, and it is correspondingly wary of simply linking its heroes with those of the classical past. In III. viii–ix we encounter a knight called Paridell, who seduces a married woman called Helenore. This action recalls, in a deliberately down-market form, the rape of Helen, which initiated the first of the great Western epic actions, the siege of Troy. Paridell's name is a jingly revision of 'Paris', who seized Helen, and Helenore is Helen all over again, a secondary, belated version of her great Homeric prototype. Paridell claims to be a dynastic hero, who carries with him the blood of Troy, and who is the literal offspring of the epic past. He proudly relates his blood-line: a stanza tells us about Paris, 'Most famous Worthy of the world' (III. ix. 34); another extols the marvels of Helen. We might expect Paridell to be the true-born offspring of these two beings from a heroic former age, who revives their virtue in the present. But, as he confesses a shade shamefacedly, he is actually descended from the union of Paris

35

with Oenone ('Whiles yet on *Ida* he a shepheard hight, | On faire *Oenone* got a louely boy' (III. ix. 36)). And, as he relates his dynastic history, it becomes less and less satisfyingly continuous:

> The which he dying left next in remaine
> To *Paridas* his sonne.
> From whom I *Paridell* by kin descend.
>
> (III. ix. 37)

The half-line here ('To *Paridas* his sonne') is like a suspicious gap in a row of family portraits: it suggests that Paridell may have done some discreet pruning of his family tree. The carefully vague phrase 'by kin descend' does not exclude the possibility that Paridell was born from the wrong side of the blanket. And his own history is a dynastic dead-end. He elopes with Helenore, and then just abandons her: 'He nould [would not] be clogd. So had he serued many one' (III. x. 35).

The audience of Paridell's dubious genealogy includes Britomart, the knight of Book III, and the dynastic heroine who will bring forth a progeny of British kings. One would expect her story to be the true type of dynastic history, as Paridell's is its antitype. But the position is not nearly so simple. Britomart naïvely asks Paridell to continue his story to take in her own ancestry, which she derives from Aeneas's son Iulus. It is from Paridell, the bastard offspring of the heroic past, that we learn how Britomart is sprung from the heroes of classical epic. And this is disturbing. Britomart takes the story straight: in delight she interrupts its dubious story-teller to praise Britain's capital as a New Troy, which revives both the blood-line and the moral qualities of Greece and Rome:

> There there (said *Britomart*) a fresh appeard
> The glory of the later world to spring,
> And *Troy* againe out of her dust was reard.
>
> (III. ix. 44)

The simple optimism of the heroine is qualified both by the setting, and by Spenser's knowledge of British history. Britain was believed by the medieval historian Geoffrey of Monmouth to have been founded by a mythological figure called Brutus, who was thought to have been a straggler from the Trojan forces who went on to found Rome. The early Tudor historian Polydore Vergil, however, discredited this historical myth, and so made it difficult for subsequent writers to claim that there were firm historical links between the empire of Rome and the history of Britain. The episode with Paridell and Britomart accommodates this historical uncertainty: it is Paridell not Spenser who implies that his Queen is the offspring of a true Trojan blood-line. Spenser is always aware that there might be an unbridgeable gap between his mythologies of the British past and what actually occurred.

As we have seen, Spenser was a 'Renaissance' poet. That is, he wishes to revive the past, but is aware that the metaphor of rebirth brings with it a corresponding mortal weakness: people live and breed; they also die and fail to have children. So to link the power of a poem to the forces of biological reproduction is at once to claim great strength and a painful weakness. And this sense of weakness runs right through the dynastic element of *The Faerie Queene*. Britomart is represented as the main agent of dynastic history in the poem, but her history is both incomplete and riven with frailty. After she has fallen in love with Arthegall's image in the magic mirror, she is urged by her nurse to visit the ancient British sorcerer Merlin, from whom she receives a prophecy of the mighty line of offspring which will emerge from her union with Arthegall. Their children will not only continue their blood line; they will continuingly revive the glories of the past:

> For from thy wombe a famous Progenie
> Shall spring, out of the auncient *Troian* blood,
> Which shall reuiue the sleeping memorie
> Of those same antique Peres, the heauens brood,
> Which *Greeke* and *Asian* riuers stained with their blood.
>
> (III. iii. 22)

This prophecy is in the grand tradition of dynastic romance, promising an endless renaissance of classical heroes through the fertile union of the heroine. Virgil's Aeneas witnesses a partial history of Rome's future when he visits his father in the underworld in Book VI of the *Aeneid*, and Ariosto's heroine Bradamante receives a similar prediction of her grand dynastic future. But Spenser's version of the dynastic prophecy is oddly dislocated. It occurs in a flashback from the main action of Book III, which relates the early life of Britomart; and it points forward to a future which we never actually witness. Britomart and

37

Arthegall never marry or have children in the poem as we have it. And the prophecy ends with significant abruptness when it reaches the reign of Queen Elizabeth ('Then shall a royall virgin raine' (III. iii. 49)):

> But yet the end is not. There *Merlin* stayd,
>   As ouercomen of the spirites powre,
>   Or other ghastly spectacle dismayd.
>
> (III. iii. 50)

Quite what Merlin sees coming after the reign of Elizabeth can never be known. But the abrupt and threatening conclusion to his prophecy makes one thing certain: the line of the British Trojans which derives from Britomart will not live on for ever. Spenser cannot quite manage to write a dynastic romance in which a royal line is presented as endlessly reviving. As a result he is drawn to abrupt and incomplete histories, histories which suggest that an endless 'revival' of a heroic past is a virtual impossibility, and that the shadow of mortality falls over even the strongest dynasty. This does not make the poem an artistic failure, however. *The Faerie Queene* offers anticipations of an ideal future, flashes of a perfect past. And, in between, its heroes strive and fail to pull these two worlds together in the present. A great part of the power of *The Faerie Queene* derives from its temporal elusiveness: we read about an antique past and a glorious future. We catch fleeting glimpses of a world which was, and of a world which is about to be. We are given a sense that a great future is at hand, and that this might be a heroic revival of past virtue. But we never rest comfortably in the present, and are never sure that the deeds we witness will in fact lead to a heroic future. A dynastic epic written to praise a virgin Queen cannot quite present the nation's history as the glorious unfolding of a biologically continuous dynasty. It cannot quite see the present as a heroic revival of past perfections. It can only try to do so, and can only see the nation's history by glimpses.

Arthur, the other major dynastic hero of the poem, also has a vision of his national history, which is also interrupted. In the House of Alma he is taken to the 'ruinous and old' room of Eumnestes (memory), where, among worm-eaten chronicles, he reads a history of Britain – until it suddenly breaks off:

> After him *Vther*, which *Pendragon* hight,
> Succeding There abruptly it did end,
> Without full point, or other Cesure right,
> As if the rest some wicked hand did rend,
> Or th'Authour selfe could not at least attend
> To finish it: that so vntimely breach
> The Prince him selfe halfe seemeth to offend,
> Yet secret pleasure did offence empeach,
> And wonder of antiquitie long stopt his speach.
>
> (II. x. 68)

The most surprising word for the mellifluous Spenser to have introduced into the language is 'abruptly'. 'Abrupt', though, is a word which came into his mind when thinking about the structure of his own poem: the Letter to Ralegh notes that 'the beginning of the whole worke seemeth abrupte' (p.737). Spenser's use of 'abruptly' in his description of Arthur's reading has etymological force: it means, literally, 'broken off'. Spenser, despite his reputation for fluency, is a master of the abrupt caesura. He is a poet who can use fragmentary forms, forms which appear to have been broken off by the corrosive power of time, to evoke a marvel. There are several half-lines in the *Aeneid*, which could indicate that Virgil's poem was incomplete, or which could be the result of what Spenser elsewhere calls 'cursed Eld' causing the text to decay. Spenser is very willing to exploit these abrupt lacunae, both to generate wonder and, like artificial distressing on reproduction antique furniture, to make his poem appear to be old enough to have been battered by time. Emotions or scenes which are beyond comprehension frequently prompt him artfully to break the flow of his verse. Belphoebe's clothes are too majestic for description, so Spenser breaks off his attempt to describe them ('and all the skirt about I Was hemd with golden fringe' (II. iii. 26) – and there the amputated alexandrine ends, without punctuation). Arthur's rudely interrupted reading of the chronicle, though, shows an even more deep-seated aspect of Spenser's art. As Arthur's reading reaches the present – he is the son of Uther – his reading stops. The old chronicle enters the present; and at that moment neither Arthur nor his chronicler can know what happens next. Dynastic history is unfinished. It leaves us with a timeless participle: 'Succeding', and then a break in a fragile, physically decayed text.

The Faerie Queene is itself unfinished, 'As if the rest some wicked hand did rend, I Or th'Authour selfe could not at least attend I To finish it' (II. x. 68). The first instalment of the poem, printed in 1590, contained Books I–III. It ended with an image of more or less perfect resolution, as Amoret is freed by Britomart from the House of Busirane, and is united with her love Sir Scudamour. The two melt together in amorous union. This original ending to Book III may well anticipate an ideal projected ending of the poem, in which all the would-be dynastic heroes of the poem would be united:

> Had ye them seene, ye would haue surely thought,
> That they had beene that faire *Hermaphrodite*,
> Which that rich *Romane* of white marble wrought.
>
> (III. xii. 46, 1590 version)

Male and female are united into a static image of fixed, hermaphroditic perfection. Only Britomart, still alone and 'halfe enuying their blesse', disturbs the closural equilibrium of the scene, and reminds us of the unfinished work which Spenser still has in hand. When Book III was reissued in 1596 along with Books IV–VI, however, its original ending was revised. The union of Scudamour and Amoret was rudely broken asunder. In the new version Britomart emerges triumphantly with Amoret from Busirane's castle, only to find that Scudamour has left in despair. Dynastic unions and resolved endings are equally elusive in the second instalment of *The Faerie Queene*, which contained Books IV–VI as well as the first three. Book VI, which ended the 1596 edition, concludes on a note of pessimistic inconclusiveness. The Blattant Beast is captured by Calidore in VI. xii. 37. In the very next stanza the Beast escapes to savage the whole world again, 'Ne spareth he the gentle Poets rime' (VI. xii. 40). Spenser was drawn increasingly to represent continuing processes rather than endings, unending battles rather than victories.

In the edition of *The Faerie Queene* published posthumously in 1609 there appeared for the first time 'Two Cantos of Mutabilitie: which, both for Forme and Matter, appeare to be parcell of some following Booke of *The Faerie Queene*, under the Legend of Constancie'. The relation between these two cantos (numbered vi and vii) with their final, prayerful, two stanzas (called, 'The viii. Canto, unperfite'), and the rest of the poem has been much

40

debated. The cantos treat one of the major themes of the poem: change. The titaness Mutabilitie claims that she governs the whole world and attempts to win sovereignty from Jove. Her case is referred to the judgement of Nature, who witnesses a pageant of the seasons which is supposed to illustrate the complete control which Mutabilitie has over the universe. But Nature concludes her judgement by finding that a greater force than Mutabilitie is at work in the world, and that change is directed towards an ultimate goal:

> I well consider all that ye haue sayd,
>   And find that all things stedfastnes doe hate
>   And changed be: yet being rightly wayd
>   They are not changed from their first estate;
>   But by their change their being doe dilate:
>   And turning to themselues at length againe,
>   Doe worke their owne perfection so by fate:
>   Then ouer them Change doth not rule and raigne;
> But they raigne ouer change, and doe their states maintaine.

(VII. vii. 58)

The Mutabilitie Cantos may just be an incomplete fragment of an unfinished book, which descended to the printer Matthew Lownes when he inherited the papers of William Ponsonby, Spenser's chief printer, along with his business. Lownes could possibly have printed them to make his 1609 edition more attractive to the book-buying public. But they could also represent Spenser's deliberate attempt to end his poem 'abruptly', as it were, with an incomplete book, which would reflect the power of time to erode the works of mortality. Ariosto also left behind him five cantos which appear to be part of an incompletely revised version of *Orlando furioso*. The Mutabilitie Cantos mark Spenser's poem not as an epic about the power of a human hero to shape a nation, or about the power of a poet to revive the heroic past in new, living images of virtue, but as an epic of mortality, in which heroes and poets alike are contained within a process of change. And they mark Spenser as a poet whose greatness is intimately linked to his ability to ride out the forces which controlled him. 'The viii. Canto, unperfite', which follows Nature's judgement and is the last we have of the poem, contains only two stanzas of prayer. The poem ends 'abruptly', broken off, on a note of humility. Its poet is no longer the epic 'maker' who can shape a

41

fiction from the history of his nation, but a man subjected to the changeful, eroding, but finally – perhaps – reviving power of time:

> Then gin I thinke on that which Nature sayd,
>> Of that same time when no more *Change* shall be,
>> But stedfast rest of all things firmely stayd
>> Vpon the pillours of Eternity,
>> That is contrayr to *Mutabilitie*:
>> For, all that moueth, doth in *Change* delight:
>> But thence-forth all shall rest eternally
>> With Him that is the God of Sabbaoth hight:
> O that great Sabbaoth God, graunt me that Sabaoths sight.
>
> (VII. viii. 2)

No lines in sixteenth-century poetry are more moving than these. Prayers should acknowledge in their form their vanity, since it is only by doing so that they show their dependence on a superior power. This stanza, smoothly moving, has a strangely irresolved syntax: it does not quite have the impetus to move to a rousing conclusion. Its opening leads us to expect that *after* musing on the words of Nature, Spenser will append some conclusion of his own: it should, as it were, read 'Then gin I thinke... And then conclude'. The maker's voice subsides instead into an invocation to a superior power. An epic of mortality should end like this, abruptly broken off, with a prayer to transcend the limits of the flesh. Whether Spenser intended it to do so, or whether the fact that it does so is owing to the action of 'cursed Eld', we shall never know.

4

Allegorical Epic

Spenser describes *The Faerie Queene* in the Letter to Ralegh as 'a continued Allegory, or darke conceit' (p. 737). Allegory can be a demon in the mind of would-be readers of the poem. It is tempting to regard an allegory as a code which presses for a one-to-one correspondence between a fictional event – say, Arthegall's conquest of Grantorto in Book V – and a single referent, such as the defeat of the Spanish Armada. This belief can only make *The Faerie Queene* frustrating to read: if one thinks there is a simple key to the allegory, and that one does not have it, one can feel locked in. Allegory, however, is not a single mode of writing, but a hybrid of several different modes of signifying. And this hybrid form is usually less concerned with making single relations between particular stories and particular meanings than with extending and exploring complex ideas. Many medieval allegorical poems are what might be called 'conceptual' allegories. That is, they take a central concept and explore its ramifications. Chaucer's *House of Fame*, for example, takes the concept 'fame' and explores the range of its meanings – from 'rumour' to 'glory' to 'reputation'. It uses a variety of episodes to illustrate each of these ambiguously interpenetrating aspects of the word. A favourite trick of Langland's long allegorical dream poem *Piers Plowman* is to meditate on an ambiguous term such as 'meed' (which can mean 'reward' or 'bribe') and to generate stories and exempla of its various aspects. At the end of these poems the central terms on which they brood have been not so much defined as de-fined: they have been stretched and extended into something unsettlingly complex. Their meaning can be enacted only through a number of interlocking senses and a variety of alternative narratives. Allegory of this kind changes and enriches the language, and is close kin to fiction, which through complex

43

narrative opens up new spaces for thoughts which lie beyond the limits of individual words.

Allegorical habits of mind can be traced right down into the syntax of *The Faerie Queene*. Classical rhetoricians such as Quintilian defined the trope 'allegoria' as no more than a continued metaphor, such as 'The ship of state foundered on the rocks of inflation'. This kind of writing occupies the middle ground between what we now might call metaphor and fiction: it adopts the transposition of attributes which is characteristic of metaphor (states, like ships, sometimes founder), but it retains the consistency of grammatical forms which most people would regard as being a necessary part of fiction: the ship of state is, so to speak, a consistent character through the allegory. Spenser very often straddles the flexible boundary between these modes of writing. Abstract nouns in *The Faerie Queene* often have an unusual amount of life to them, and one of the pleasures of the poem comes from treading the slippery boundary between allegory and metaphor. This is an area of darkness, which Spenser often uses to evoke dingy emotions. Florimell, imprisoned in Proteus's under-sea den, is beset by fears which do not have the substantial life of personifications:

> And in the midst thereof did horror dwell,
> And darkenesse dredd, that neuer viewed day.

> (IV. xi. 4)

Part of the horror here is that no one called 'Horror' or 'Darkenesse' is present. The semi-personification suits the imprisoning setting perfectly: there might be allegorical monsters out there, but they are only visible out of the corner of Florimell's fearful eye. 'Feare' is often given enough personified energy to pursue a character in *The Faerie Queene* (the Souldan's forces flee 'High ouer hilles, and lowly ouer dales, | As they were follow'd of their former feare' (V. viii. 39)), but never becomes real enough to fight. And this indicates the brilliant suggestiveness of Spenser's allegorical writing: part of what is frightening about fear is that it is never simply related to an object, that it is never quite there. Spenser makes similar use of muscular abstract nouns, which just fail to become personifications, throughout the poem. When Guyon enters the Bowre of Blisse and sees the naked maidens who bathe there 'His stubborne brest gan secret pleasaunce to embrace' (II. xii. 65). Not Secret Pleasaunce, and not a literal embrace, since that would render a flicker of rebellious lust too corporeal. The allegory is held just below the literal surface of the description, as Guyon tries to hold the unusual turbulence of his breast in check. The next level up, so to speak, of allegory is outright personification allegory. This might seem like a very simple matter of turning an abstract noun into a person or thing. On the face of it this could be expected to go with the grain of the language, rather than against it: Fear cannot be anything other than fearful. Sleep, in Ovid's *Metamorphoses*, is so sleepy that he has continually to shake himself off himself. Spenser's personifications *can* be mechanical. When, in his allegorical representation of the human body, the House of Alma, he proudly says that 'The maister Cooke was cald *Concoction*' (i.e. digestion (II. ix. 31)), it is hard to hold back a groan. But the best moments of personification allegory are sources of surprise. Medieval allegorical writing frequently postpones the naming of a personification until after it is described, so that the reader undergoes a testing preliminary search for the name of the abstraction which they have seen, before the author obligingly reveals it. The name, once revealed, retains the uncertainty of the preliminary search for it. This is a staple of Spenserian allegory. In Book IV Sir Scudamour has lost Amoret, his love. He comes to a cottage, set in 'the mouldred earth', which seems to be a smithy, occupied by a blacksmith:

> Rude was his garment, and to rags all rent,
> Ne better had he, ne for better cared:
> With blistred hands emongst the cinders brent,
> And fingers filthie, with long nayles vnpared,
> Right fit to rend the food, on which he fared.

(IV. v. 35)

All seems like a literal blacksmith, until that odd detail that his nails are long. People who hammer iron might be expected to have short and cracked nails. It is a signal that something more than literal is occurring. The next line is 'His name was *Care*'. The name is extremely difficult to predict, especially since Care is explicitly described as care*less* in the second line of the extract just quoted. But when the name comes it is exactly right: it marks an extraordinary overlap between the mental world of a courtly lover and the obsessive labour of a rural artisan, an artisan who worries so much that he ceases to care for himself. The term is stretched in order to unite several different worlds of experience.

45

The ultimate horror of personification allegory is contact with the unnamable. This occurs only once in the poem, when a rudely sylvan character with pendulous ears and an enormous red nose ravishes Amoret. The Argument to the Canto (IV. vii) refers to him as 'lust' (lower-case letters are used, and, given that Spenser was in England to oversee the printing of the poem, these have some standing), and he is immediately identified as Lust by most readers – that nose, after all, is something of a warning signal. *The Faerie Queene* is a poem which attempts to shape love into a decorous, procreative form, and so Lust, the unnamable obscenity, is its ultimate enemy. The character (to deprive him of his name) also shows one way in which allegory can involve sudden shifts of gear between different kinds of fiction. Æmylia is also imprisoned along with Amoret. She tells how she became captive to the carle (churl) in a story which looks at first like the kind of realistic novella which Ariosto frequently inserted into his poem. Æmylia tells how she intended to elope with a Squire of Low Degree. At their rendezvous she meets, not her lover, but the unnamed figure (IV. vii. 18). The personification disrupts, but at the same time comments indirectly upon, the literal fiction: his abrupt entrance intimates that elopements without the secure bonds of marriage are likely to lead to unpleasant contact with nasty swollen things, things which imprison and destroy.

Personifications in Spenser are not just externalized demons, whom the heroes must avoid or kill. They can drift inconspicuously into the minds of those who encounter them. Despaire does not simply meet Redcrosse and do despairing things; he is a threatening adversary because he so very nearly metamorphoses from Despaire into despair. His voice hauntingly fades into that of the hero:

> The knight much wondred at his suddeine wit,
>> And said, The terme of life is limited,
>> Ne may a man prolong, nor shorten it;
>> The souldier may not moue from watchfull sted,
>> Nor leaue his stand, vntill his Captaine bed.
>> Who life did limit by almightie doome,
>> (Quoth he) knowes best the termes established;
>> And he, that points the Centonell his roome,
> Doth license him depart at sound of morning droome.

(I. ix. 41)

Despaire is trying to persuade Redcrosse that he is damned by using the orthodox Calvinist belief that no human action can ever merit salvation, but suppressing the equally orthodox belief that the grace of God will save a number of the elect. Redcrosse's last word here, 'bed' (bid), is a rousing command of a martial hero who will resist the counsels of despair; but the word is also that of someone who is crumpling into despair – who quite fancies a spell in bed. In the next line ('Who life did limit...') it is for a moment unclear who is speaking, as the knight's voice blurs over into that of Despaire. Holinesse is being led by its own kind of argument – that all human actions are the products of a fallen nature and therefore can never merit salvation – to despair.

Simple personifications in Spenser always denote danger, and the chief danger they represent is that of simplification. The heroes and heroines of each book represent complex and multi-faceted virtues. Very often their virtues include within themselves propensities to certain kinds of vice (Guyon is prone to over-rigorous resistance to all forms of pleasure, particularly of a sexual kind; Sir Calidore, the knight of Courtesy, is prone to substitute generous passivity for action; Arthegall, the knight of Justice, tends to a hard-edged legalism). An ideal image of virtue is something for which Spenser, his heroes, and his readers are always searching; but the closer we get to it, the more complicated and distant it appears to be. 'Holinesse' is never directly manifested by a single action of the Redcrosse Knight; rather, it is a property which is worked towards in the whole process of his story. For all Spenser's knights the chief danger is that of reducing the complexity of their task – which is to realize the fullest and often the most ambiguous aspects of their virtues – to a simple formula. To become a personification – a simple, flat representation of an unambiguous state of mind – is in Spenser's world quite possible. But it is a desperate horror, not the goal, but the enemy of his kind of complicating allegory. Only one character in *The Faerie Queene* does turn into a personification. In Book III Britomart rests at Malbecco's castle. It is a world of simple fabliau, in which a *senex amans* (old man in love) is desperate to prevent his desirable and desiring young wife Helenore from eloping, like her more famous namesake Helen of Troy, with a younger man. She does elope with Paridell, though, and ends her days in the company of the lustful satyrs. Malbecco witnesses her adulteries

('Nine times he heard him come aloft ere day' (III. x. 48)), and is transformed into a principle of dynamic simplicity, Jealousy:

> But through long anguish, and selfe-murdring thought
> He was so wasted and forepined quight,
> That all his substance was consum'd to nought,
> And nothing left, but like an aery Spright,
> That on the rockes he fell so flit and light,
> That he thereby receiu'd no hurt at all,
> But chaunced on a craggy cliff to light;
> Whence he with crooked clawes so long did crall,
> That at the last he found a caue with entrance small.
>
> . . . .
>
> Where he through priuy griefe, and horrour vaine,
> Is woxen so deform'd, that he has quight
> Forgot he was a man, and Gealosie is hight.

                                                    (III. x. 57–60)

Spenser's allegorical figures often inhabit abandoned places, which they permeate with their spirit, and which reciprocally cast dark light on the significance of their occupants. Errour lurks in a wood; Care moulders in a copse; Despaire lives on in a cave. Malbecco joins these solitaries in a dry and infertile place. Britomart's task is to brave the perplexing complexity of love; Malbecco effectively writes himself out of the complex allegory of love in Book III by choosing to be dominated by only one of its aspects.

Creatures in abandoned places or woods (at least in the early stages of the poem) often try to tempt knights into exploring one aspect of their virtue at the expense of the others. Spenser's knights also enter places of instruction, such as the House of Holiness in I. x, or the House of Alma in II. ix-x, which tend to focus a variety of personified virtues in a single place. The poem also contains places which offer visions of perfection, such as the Garden of Adonis in III. vi, the Temple of Venus in IV. x, the Temple of Isis in V. vii, or Mount Acidale, on which Sir Calidore sees Colin Clout piping to the Graces, in VI. x. These locations are usually marked by a spatial (and often circular) arrangement of virtues, rather than a sequential parade of vices; in the Temple of Venus Amoret sits in the centre of Womanhood, Shamefastnesse, Cherefulnesse, Modestie, Curtesie, Silence, and Obedience, focusing all these restrictive feminine virtues in a single spot. In the House of Pride and the Castle of Busirane – both of which

48

seek to entrap Spenser's heroes – vices parade in sequence, each usurping centre stage for a moment. This difference is critical: for Spenser, goodness is virtually identifiable with a rich union of differing principles. An object situated 'in the midst' of a surrounding body of abstractions, or of a surrounding landscape, is almost always richly significant, and, in the moral scheme of the poem, is almost always good.

A further element in allegorical writing is its willingness to bring together different time schemes. Early commentators on the Bible developed a way of reconciling the very different kinds of fiction presented in the Old and New Testaments, which involved seeing the life of Christ as the typological fulfilment of actions which occurred in the Old Testament. The Old Testament story of how God gives Abraham a ram to prevent his having to sacrifice his son Isaac, when read 'typologically', would prefigure the sacrifice of the lamb of God (Christ) for mankind. Typology is a continuing part of allegorical writing. In *The Faerie Queene* it is most to the fore in Book I – although even here it is not consistently in play. Spenser's best historical allegories create actions of sufficient complexity to be related to a number of events in the histories of nations and of people at once. They have the excitement produced by a perilous coincidence of many areas of interest in one point. In Book I there are continual chiming overlaps between the history of a Christian knight (and the influential humanist Desiderius Erasmus in his *Handbook of a Christian Knight* made that term one which could be applied to any Christian) and that of the English Church in the sixteenth century. To escape from Duessa, the duplicitous twin of the true Una, is the chief goal of Redcrosse. Duessa has unmissable overtones of the Whore of Babylon as described in the Book of Revelation 17: she is given a Beast to ride, a purple garment and a papal triple crown in I. vii. 16–17. She is repeatedly associated with the forms of idolatry which Protestant propagandists such as the martyrologist John Foxe (1516–87) represent as being at the heart of Roman Catholicism. Redcrosse's wavering descent into Errour's den has strong correspondences with the return of England to Catholicism under Elizabeth's sister Mary; but the sliding ease with which this knight, pricking on the plain only a few stanzas before, finds himself with Errour, a dark, woodland creature of terrifying fecundity, and of a power which entangles, has resonances far beyond simple historical correspondence. The episode is part of a representation of life as a matter of repeatedly encountering unexpected adversaries in odd places, and a vision of human – and indeed poetic – labour as a continual battle with the desire to wander. Redcrosse's life of wandering ends with a final battle against the dragon in Eden. This is an apocalyptic battle between a Christ-figure and the old serpent Satan, which marks the end of time. But at the same time it is a fable about personal regeneration, in which Redcrosse is sustained, and as it were baptized, by the Waters of Life. The climax of Book I also looks forward to the destruction of the Antichrist of the Pope, another theme which is harped on unendingly in sixteenth-century English Protestant propaganda. The allegory of Book I interlinks three overlapping levels of history: personal, spiritual history is combined with the universal history of the world as it progresses towards apocalypse, and both are tied in with the national epic designs of the poem. These kinds of allegory are not all equally present at all times: the essence of allegorical writing is that it demands continual interpretive flexibility from its readers.

Views of what constitutes a nation, and of what exactly goes to make up its history, are always contentious. Spenser often uses historical allegory, not just to relate important events in the English past, but to impose his own peculiar vision on that past. *The Faerie Queene* does contain some relatively simple representations of actual historical events. Most of these are concentrated in Book V, in the later, and more weary, section of the poem, which was first published in 1596. And most are designed to put forward an aggressively Protestant view of history. The latter part of V. xi relates how a character called Bourbon gives away his shield, which allegorically presents the conversion of the French King Henry Bourbon from Protestantism to Catholicism in July 1593. A number of internal inconsistencies suggest that the episode may have been inserted into the poem very late, perhaps even as the second instalment of the poem was going to press. In V. x Spenser represents, in the story of Arthur's liberation of Belge from Geryoneo, Philip of Spain being driven out of the Low Countries by an idealized Protestant nobleman. This, though, is not a simple representation of what was happening in Europe. It harks back to the Earl of Leicester's mission to the Low Countries nearly ten years before, rather than reflecting the continual

50

waverings of the Queen's policy as it was in 1596. Spenser's historical allegory is often designed to change his world, rather than simply to reflect it. He wrote in the 1590s with a zealous nostalgia for the active Protestant interventionism associated with Leicester, Sidney, and Walsingham in the late 1570s and early 1580s. In the later parts of *The Faerie Queene* he wished to create an allegorical fiction which would transform national history, and perhaps his Queen, into something which corresponded more closely than the reality to his partisan vision of England.

To gasp this dimension of Spenser's writing we should turn to a definition of allegory which is much closer to him in time than any which have so far been considered. George Puttenham in the *Arte of English Poesie* (1589) associates allegory with the necessary double-speak which goes along with being a courtier:

the courtly figure *Allegoria* ... is when we speake one thing and thinke another, and that our wordes and our meanings meete not. The use of this figure is so large, and his virtue of so great efficacie as it is supposed no man can pleasantly utter and perswade without it, but in effect is sure never or very seldome to thrive and prosper in the world, that cannot skilfully put in ure [use], in somuch as not onely every common Courtier, but also the gravest Counsellour, yea and the most noble and wisest Prince of them all are many times enforced to use it ... Of this figure therefore which for his duplicitie we call the figure of *false semblant or dissimulation* we will speake first as of the chief ringleader and captaine of all other figures.[1]

This extraordinarily rich definition implies that allegory is something conspiratorial ('ringleaders' head bodies who do reprehensible things, according to *OED*), and that it is second cousin to the noble art of political lying. Puttenham's definition is geared to the life of a courtier, for whom strategic reserve, and, perhaps, an element of duplicity, were necessary elements in the art of survival. These qualities are vital for those who wished to counsel a reluctant monarch to take a course of action towards which they were hostile. As we have seen, Spenser was often slightly at odds with royal policy, and the historical fiction of *The Faerie Queene* is, in part, designed to refashion the Queen into an image of her as Spenser wished her to be. Spenser writes in the Letter to Ralegh appended to the 1590 edition of *The Faerie Queene* of his ambition to 'fashion a gentleman'; he also uses the same verb of his Queen, who is given a choice of exemplars against which to shape herself ('But either *Gloriana* let her chuse, | Or in *Belphœbe* fashioned to bee', (III. pr. 5)). This is not quite a Hobson's choice; but both the images from which the Queen can choose are made *for* her by the poet, and both will 'fashion', or reshape her, in their image. The poem creates a glittering shell of praise around its Queen, and urges her to grow into the shape it makes for her. It is by no means simply adulatory. Jonson notes in his 'Epistle to Master John Selden' that he has 'too oft preferr'd | Men past their termes, and prais'd some names too much, | But 'twas with purpose to have made them such' (ll. 20–2). Spenser's praise of Elizabeth serves a similar exhortatory function, to transform through eulogy. This can make his historical allegory something more than an indirect way of transcribing history: it can mean that the poem treads a perilous but thrilling line between history as Spenser wished it to be, history as it was, and history as his Queen and her ministers wanted it to be. A case in point is the story which occupies IV. vii-viii, in which Arthur's Squire, Timias, is found by the chaste Belphoebe tending the wounds of Amoret. She exits with an angry question, spat out so fast that there is no time for a question-mark: 'Is this the faith, she said, and said no more' (IV. vii. 36). This is an allegorical image of the fall of Queen Elizabeth's favourite Sir Walter Ralegh, who lost the Queen's affections when he married one of her maids of honour, Elizabeth Throckmorton, in 1592. Spenser, however, blends historical allegory into wish-fulfilment: Belphoebe and Timias are subsequently reunited by a dove (a frail intermediary which could almost represent the healing influence of Spenser's own fiction), despite the fact that by 1596 the real Ralegh had not regained the full extent of his former favour.

The best example of the perilous balance of Spenser's historical allegory occurs in V. x, when Spenser describes Mercilla's arraignment of Duessa. This represents Elizabeth's ostentatiously reluctant trial of her cousin and Roman Catholic rival to the throne of England, Mary Queen of Scots, in 1586. The episode appears at first to present an unequivocally laudatory portrait of the Queen, surrounded in clouds of glory and framed by throngs of angels, and all but indescribably majestic:

All ouer her a cloth of state was spred,
Not of rich tissew, nor of cloth of gold,
Nor of ought else, that may be richest red,
But like a cloud, as likest may be told,
That her brode spreading wings did wyde vnfold;
Whose skirts were bordred with bright sunny beams,
Glistring like gold, amongst the plights enrold,
And here and there shooting forth siluer streames,
Mongst which crept little Angels through the glittering gleames.

(V. ix. 28)

When Spenser writes of allegory he always talks of veils and clouds. In the Letter to Ralegh the poem is described as being 'clowdily enwrapped in Allegoricall devises' (p.737). Mercilla is so enwrapped in clouds of obscuring allegory that she is scarcely visible at all. Does 'whose skirts' refer to Mercilla, or to the clouds which surround her? And the cloth of state under which she is concealed is described chiefly by comparison with what it is not like. The effect is of a poet who is so dazzled by perfection that he cannot bring himself to look at what he sees. This vision of merciful majesty is entirely in keeping with Elizabeth I's widely established public image of herself as a magnificently pitiful woman. This reputation, however, is qualified by what happens in the Mercilla episode, in which Spenser's pitiful heroine does not simply dispense mercy, as her name would suggest. She is urged by her male and zealously Protestant counsellors to condemn Duessa to death, despite her pitiful tears. In the silent space between the end of Canto x and the start of Canto xi, Duessa is executed. Without violating the carefully cultivated public image of his Queen as a woman disposed to pity, Spenser represents her as a ruler who values justice over mercy, and who follows the advice of her male counsellors.

The structure of the poem can play a part in the courtly and insinuating aspect of its allegory too. One way of speaking one thing and meaning another is to make apparently innocent conjunctions of different strands of a fiction, which, to a knowing reader, strike off sparks of unspoken significance from each other. The description of Mercilla's trial of Duessa is immediately preceded by a description of the poet Bonfont (or Malfont, as he becomes) whose tongue is 'Nayld to a post, adiudged so by law' (V. ix. 25). The relation between this episode and Mercilla's trial of

Duessa is not spelt out by the poet. It could innocently suggest that no one but a villain can speak anything but good of the magnificent Mercilla. But it might also be a piece of structural double-speak: as the poet attempts his closest presentation of his Queen, he has to watch his own tongue, and be careful to throw out a cloud of praise, before he intimates that mercy might not be the best course of action for a Protestant monarch. Allegory, as Puttenham defines it, is a mode in which 'our wordes and our meanings meete not'. In Spenser's hands it becomes a mode of signifying which is as versatile as fiction: it requires of its readers as of its author a flexible willingness to pursue implicit suggestion; and it presents its readers not with simple, fixed meanings, but with a wealth of all but ungraspable suggestion.

5

Heroes and Villains and Things in Between

The professed end of *The Faerie Queene*, as set out in the Letter to Ralegh, is 'to fashion a gentleman or noble person in vertuous and gentle discipline' (p.737). The verb 'to fashion' suggests a continuing process of reshaping and of education, which might extend both to characters within the text and to its readers. *The Faerie Queene* does not simply instantiate moral virtues, since its form of allegory continually complicates our perceptions of what a given virtue is. Rather, the poem invites its readers to reflect on the relations between the chief virtue on trial in the book, and the episode before them. Each book is headed 'The Legend of Sir [name]. Or of [virtue]', and this syntactic form does not explicitly state that, say, Guyon is identified with Temperance, or Arthegall with Justice (although in the Letter to Ralegh Spenser comes much closer to making that identification). Each book relates a set of stories about a knight, which explore a virtue. And the knights often explore the virtue through negative, or testingly near negative, example. Guyon, the hero of the Book of Temperance, is tempted to descend into the Cave of Mamon. He manifests one version of temperance by abstaining from the food he is offered by his rust-covered host, and by refusing the hand of the proud Philotime (whose name means love of glory). But when he emerges back into 'this vitall aire' he faints at once (II. vii. 66). Guyon's faint cannot be simply decoded, but it suggests that the hero has manifested a kind of temperance which is perilously close to self-destructive abstinence. Guyon is particularly prone to interpret his virtue narrowly. In the climactic episode of Book II he voyages to the Bowre of Blisse, past a mass of temptations to digress from his task. He ignores pitiful ladies who cry for his help – and whom a traditional chivalric hero from Ariosto would have instinctively paused to assist – and sternly, and more than a shade discourteously, hurls to the ground the cup which Excesse offers to him. 'Temperance' is a complex term. It can signify 'the ability to moderate the appetite', which brings it close in meaning to 'abstinence'. But for Aristotle it signifies the ability to follow a mean between extremes, and it can also mean 'a mixture of properties or attributes' – a sense which vestigially survives in the way we still talk of someone's 'temper', or the mixture of qualities which makes them as they are. Set against these varied definitions of temperance, Guyon, by the end of his book, has become perhaps suspiciously unmixed. Most readers have responded with unease to his final destruction of the Bowre of Blisse with 'rigour pittilesse':

> But all those pleasant bowres and Pallace braue,
> *Guyon* broke downe, with rigour pittilesse;
> Ne ought their goodly workmanship might saue
> Them from the tempest of his wrathfulnesse,
> But that their blisse he turn'd to balefulnesse:
> Their groues he feld, their gardins did deface,
> Their arbers spoyle, their Cabinets suppresse,
> Their banket houses burne, their buildings race,
> And of the fairest late, now made the fowlest place.

> (II. xii. 83)

The rhetorical patterning of this stanza evokes relentless extremity rather than temperate moderation. The repetition at the start and the middle of the line of 'their' marks the repeated hammer blows of Guyon's wrath. And the antitheses (blisse/balefulness, fairest/foulest) suggest that the knight is oscillating between extremes rather than temperately pursuing an ideal path between them. Earlier critics saw the destruction of the Bowre of Blisse as marking a rush of image-breaking Puritanism to Spenser's poetical heart, as the moralist in him rebelled against the sensuousness of his own artistry. Perhaps, though, the most disturbing feature of Guyon's destruction of the Bowre is the fact that the object of his destructive wrathfulness is twice described as representing a form of temperance. The heavens protect the inmates of the Bowre from 'scorching heat' and 'cold *intemperate*', and

the milde aire with season moderate
Gently *attempred*, and disposd so well,
That still it breathed forth sweet spirit and holesome smell.

(II. xii. 51)

The Bowre of Blisse episode shows a recurrent feature of Spenser's heroes: they often are shown fighting over the outer limits of their virtue. This means that many of their strongest conflicts are with creatures or locations which could conceivably form part of the virtue which they are exploring, and which could also be aspects of themselves. Their enemies are intimately, though often also parodically, twinned with themselves. Guyon ends up waging a war against a 'Gently attempred' version of his own virtue.

A central part of the experience of reading *The Faerie Queene* is a growing impression that what seem at first to be opposites have a great deal in common. The poem insistently pairs its characters: the virtuous Florimell is twinned with a deceptively False Florimell made of snow. The saintly Una is paired with, and, at a first glance, could be confused with, the duplicitous Duessa. This can lead to unsettlingly intimate associations between heroes and their adversaries, associations which are continually reinforced by Spenser's tendency to repeat key phrases from descriptions of heroes or beneficent locations at moments when he is describing threatening people or places. The poem needs to be read in long sessions, so that a reader can catch the continuing internal echoes which run through it. These are never accidental, and do not just provide clues as to how to respond to a particular episode; they collectively build up a distinctive vision of a world in which good and bad are shown to be interdependent, in which each needs the other in order to define itself. A reader who blinks from the task of comparing one type of experience with another can be pulled into darkness and deceit.

The chief hero of *The Faerie Queene* is Prince Arthur, who is said in the Letter to Ralegh to enfold all the subsidiary virtues of the lesser knights into himself. Arthur intervenes in each book to help its titular hero, and, as the ultimate British royal hero, was probably envisaged, at an early stage of the composition of the poem, as the dynastic partner of Gloriana. Spenser's first description of Arthur in I. vii illustrates a further feature of the heroes of *The Faerie Queene*: they are designed as much to stun the reader and their adversaries as to manifest a virtue. Spenser's heroes usually flash painfully out of the darkness, and, like his personifications, are usually described before their identities are revealed, so a reader has to grope through their dazzlement to interpret what they see. Britomart dazzles before her name is known, and Arthur shines from a distance like the sun: 'His glitterand armour shined farre away, I Like glauncing light of *Phœbus* brightest ray' (I. vii. 29). He grows from a glimmer in the distance into a being with apocalyptic power, whose concealed shield shines with destructive energy: 'Men into stones therewith he could transmew, I And stones to dust, and dust to nought at all' (I. vii. 35). His capacity to generate fear is apparent in his dress, which is capped by a dragon helmet:

> His haughtie helmet, horrid all with gold,
>   Both glorious brightnesse, and great terrour bred;
>   For all the crest a Dragon did enfold
>   With greedie pawes, and ouer all did spred
>   His golden wings.
>
> (I. vii. 31)

The 'terrour', the 'greedie pawes', mark Arthur as a hero who horrifies, both in the etymological sense of 'bristling', and in the later sense of 'causing fear'. He subsists on the boundary point where virtue and martial awe coincide.

But his helmet also indicates that even Arthur has his unheroic twins. He has a 'bunch of haires discolourd diuersly' at his helmet's top. This directly recalls the headgear which the arch-enemy Archimago dons when he is impersonating Redcrosse, which also has 'A bounch of haires discolourd diuersly' (I. ii. 11) on its summit. The parallel shows the tricks which Spenser's twinning imagination plays with his readers – and even experienced readers of the poem can be misled by its continual pairings of type and antitype: A. C. Hamilton's edition notes the parallel between the two helmets, but mistakenly says that the earlier description was of Redcrosse, rather than of Archimago. The literary origins of Arthur's helmet point to another disturbing aspect of Spenserian heroism, since its chief literary prototypes all belong not to epic heroes, but to their adversaries. In Tasso's *Gerusalemme liberata* the raging pagan Soldan, leader of the forces who hold Jerusalem, wears a similarly bedragoned headpiece. And in Virgil's *Aeneid* it is not the hero Aeneas, but his wrathful enemy Turnus, who wears a dragon helmet. These allusions point to Spenser's willingness to make distracting parallels between the good and the bad, but also indicate one of his major innovations in sixteenth century epic. His heroes are men who are capable of rage – who, like Guyon with his 'rigour pittilesse', can harness the destructive power of anger to the services of virtue. Anger has been a subject of heroic song since Homer began the *Iliad* by asking his muse to sing of the wrath of Achilles, but many writers of Christian epic found it hard to appreciate the moral value of rage, since the personal virtues advocated in the New Testament are mostly mild. St Paul values charity and love over qualities which would lead to combat and destruction. Many Christian commentators on the *Aeneid* found its hero's final execution of Turnus in a burst of fury a source of unease; and many writers of Christian epic, including Ariosto, had tended to make, not their heroes, but their pagan enemies into men driven by wrath and revenge. Tasso, however, had made many of his heroes subject to noble *sdegno*, or disdain, and had made their propensity to anger part of what made them able to perform their Christian mission of liberating Jerusalem. There are plentiful prototypes too for an anger which is just and destructive in the punitive wrath of the Old Testament God. Spenser goes a step further than Tasso towards founding a heroic ideal on a kind of rage which has Judaeo-Christian prototypes. He frequently links his heroes' bursts of rage with biblical example: when he talks of the 'tempest' of Guyon's wrathfulness he is alluding to 2 Kings 23: 13–14; and his description of the destructive energy of Arthur's shield is rooted in the Apocalypse of St John, in which a wrathful God destroys the ungodly. In the last of the *Fowre Hymnes* (1596), 'An Hymne of Heavenly Beautie', Spenser presents an image of God which emphasizes 'the rigour of his judgement just' (l.158) and 'The instruments of his avenging yre' (l.182). This is Spenser's only extended representation of God, and it is a God shadowed with wrath, whose Heavenly Beautie prompts not pitiful affection, but awe:

> But lowly fall before his mercie seate,
> Close covered with the Lambes integrity,
> From the just wrath of his avengefull threate,
> That sits upon the righteous throne on hy.

(ll.148–51)

Spenser's valorizing of heroic rage in *The Faerie Queene* also has a polemical edge to it. As I suggested in the last chapter, Spenser's allegory aims to participate in and to shape history, and to enact in fictive form the views of a militant Protestant faction. The poem is consistently hostile to pity: almost always when a knight feels ruth for a helpless lady it leads him to be ensnared or delayed. Spenser wishes to portray a kind of heroism which is active, martial, and interventionist, and which is not drawn off course by compassion, or by its close Spenserian twin, sexual desire, and he wishes to present this form of militant activism to his pitiful Queen as the true form of virtue. When Redcrosse is 'inflam'd with wrath' (I. xi. 39) against the dragon, or when Arthur shakes off 'pitty deare' in order to rend down the door of Orgoglio's prison with 'furious force' (I. viii. 39), there is more at stake than a simple passion. Spenser's form of active, interventionist Protestantism is at these moments extending its roots into the veins of his heroes. Their wrathfulness creates continual and continually exciting tensions between the moral allegory and Spenser's historical designs. When the hero of the Legend of Temperance destroys the Bowre of Blisse with 'rigour pittilesse', Spenser's polemical advocacy of destructive wrath has come into direct conflict with his interest in the nature of self-regulation.

Protestantism also accounts in part for the poem's extraordinary willingness to twin images of good and bad. After Henry VIII's breach with Rome in 1535, a major task facing apologists for the English Church was to define their religion in opposition to Roman Catholicism. Early Protestant writers such as John Foxe – whose *Actes and Monuments*, familiarly known as the *Book of Martyrs* (first printed in English in 1563), was kept in every Church in the land – represented the history of religion in England as having been driven by a battle between two churches: the true, Protestant church, which had its roots in the Lollard martyrs of the fifteenth century, and the false, idolatrous church of Rome. The imaginative debt which Spenser's poem owes to this vision of history is enormous. *The Faerie Queene* contains a whole class of image-makers and idolators, who forge deceptive doubles of virtue. In the very early stages of Book I Redcrosse encounters Archimago, who, as his name suggests, is a maker of images, and who is relentlessly associated with the idolatries of the Catholic Church. Archimago fashions a phantasm which has the same shape as Redcrosse's lady Una. It enters the dreams of the knight with a seductive reality, and makes him believe that his lady is unfaithful. Archimago is presented, not just as an idolator, but also as a kind of poet, who is delighted with his own artifice:

> The maker selfe for all his wondrous witt,
> Was nigh beguiled with so goodly sight.

(I. i. 45)

As Puttenham put it in the first sentence of his *Arte of English Poesie*, 'A poet is as much to say as a maker'. The Archimago episode reflects a widespread uncertainty among Protestant writers about the powers and proper limits of a poet's imagination, which was fuelled by a fear that a poet might be doing no more than fashioning specious icons of the truth, rather than representing its true essence. Sir Philip Sidney in his *Apology for Poetry* (printed in 1595, but probably written c.1583) attempts to address this fear by making a distinction (derived from Plato) between the 'phantastike' imagination – which simply re-combines sense impressions to create strange hybrids such as centaurs – and the 'eikastike' imagination, which creates images of the good.[1] The 'eikastike' imagination can, on Sidney's view, assist in the morally elevating function of literature by presenting images of virtue so energetically that a reader is prompted to emulate them. But Sidney cannot completely persuade himself that the imagination is unequivocally valuable: he frequently uses the word 'imaginative' in a pejorative sense. Spenser shares Sidney's equivocal attitude to the mental faculty which makes his poem: *The Faerie Queene* contains continual slight signs that he fears he could be, like Archimago, no more than a maker of delusive images, who is beguiled by the likeness his own art has with truth.

Spenser's uneasiness with the sources of his own poem creates a work which is in rich and disturbing sympathy with its own enemies, and which is continually aware of negative versions of its own art. In III. viii. 5 a witch creates a false version of Florimell out of snow, replicating Spenser's own ability to generate duplicitous twins of goodness: 'She there deuiz'd a wondrous worke to frame, I Whose like on earth was neuer framed yit' – and the verb 'to frame' is often used by Spenser of his own poetic labour. The False Florimell is an elaborate robot, driven by spirits

61

who can make her eyes roll seductively and her behaviour mimic that of a flirtatious woman. She is also a living poetic conceit: her hair, like that of a Petrarchan mistress in an Elizabethan sonnet sequence, is made of golden wire; her eyes are made of burning lamps. She is a parody of the power of poetry to bring dead objects to life: 'in the stead | Of life, she put a Spright to rule the carkasse dead' (III. viii. 7).

Two of the strongest words in *The Faerie Queene* are 'antique' and 'reuiue', both of which are words which greatly expanded their range of significance in the sixteenth century in ways which indicate how during that period there emerged a growing vocabulary for expressing historical and cultural distance from the past. Spenser consciously set about to revive the antique, to make old poems live again, and this ambition draws him into a disturbing affinity with the maker of the False Florimell, who makes a dead thing come to life. In Book IV Spenser attempts to complete Chaucer's unfinished *Squire's Tale*, which he, like many others in the Renaissance, regarded as the earliest attempt to write an epic romance. Chaucer's tale is thought by some modern critics to have been left unfinished deliberately, in order to evoke the enthusiastic incompetence of the Squire, its teller, who assembles far too many magical props in the first 600 lines of the poem ever to be able to bring them together. Spenser, though, believed the poem had been completed, but that its ending had been lost by the action of 'wicked Time that all good thoughts doth waste':

> O cursed Eld the cankerworme of writs,
> How may these rimes, so rude as doth appeare,
> Hope to endure, sith workes of heavenly wits
> Are quite deuourd, and brought to nought by little bits?
>
> (IV. ii. 33)

This dead and partly destroyed poem makes Spenser think of bringing about a fragile rebirth. He begs of Chaucer's ghost 'That I thy labours lost may thus *reuiue* | And steale from thee the meede of thy due merit... through infusion sweete | Of thine owne spirit' (IV. ii. 34). He seeks to make the antique fragments of the *Squire's Tale* live again, in full awareness that his poem will, for all the transfused energy of Chaucer, be as frail as its medieval forebear. 'These rhymes' are as likely to be devoured as those of Chaucer. Spenser's continuation of the *Squire's Tale* is not only a revival of Chaucer's tale, but also a story *about* revival, which intimates that the heroes of his tale will have a revived vitality which is greater than that of its original. Spenser's version of the tale relates how Triamond received the souls of his two brothers when they died by a process of infusion. This process of endless revival is evoked by the vegetative imagery which played so strong a part in *The Shepheardes Calender*. Priamond, the first brother, dies 'Like an old Oke whose pith and sap is seare' (IV. iii. 9); Cambell, thanks to his magic ring, revives 'Like as a withered tree through husband's toyle I Is often seene full freshly to haue florisht' (IV. iii. 29). This story, like *The Shepheardes Calender* before it, is steeped in both the energies and melancholies of the year. In a Renaissance poem, a poem which seeks to revive a lost past, life and death feed each other endlessly: heroes are vital, and capable of revival and rebirth.

The revival of the dead is, however, not a straightforwardly good thing in *The Faerie Queene*. Spenser's restlessly generative imagination creates a whole breed of creatures who parody his own efforts to regenerate the dead. In I.v Night attempts to persuade the surgeon god Aesculapius to revive her nephew Sansioy after his wounding by Redcrosse. Aesculapius has a power to bring the dead to life, and for this reason was constrained by Jove to live the life of the undying in Hell:

> Such wondrous science in mans wit to raine
> When *Ioue* auizd, that could the dead reuiue,
> And fates expired could renew againe,
> Of endlesse life he might him not depriue,
> But vnto hell did thrust him downe aliue.
>
> (I. v. 40)

Aesculapius is the first of a whole string of characters in the poem who cannot die, and whose life is spent in an endless sequence of little deaths followed by parodic rebirths. The most memorable characters in Spenser's poem stare out from the page with hollow eyes, as they fade desperately away to nothing, and yet cannot relinquish their hold on life. Despaire's 'raw-bone cheekes through penurie and pine, I Were shronke into his iawes, as he did neuer dine' (I. ix. 35), and once he has failed to ensnare Redcrosse he attempts to kill himself. Pyrochles in Book II rushes ablaze back into the poem after a period of absence: 'I burne, I

63

burne, I burne, then loud he cryde, I O how I burne with implacable fire.' He plunges into the Idle Lake, 'Burning in flames, yet no flames can I see, I And dying daily, daily yet reuiue' (II. vi. 44–5). This form of endlessly painful revival, of self-consuming vitality, is the Spenserian equivalent of hell; and in his one depiction of the punishments of the damned, which occurs in the Cave of Mamon, Tantalus 'daily dyde, yet neuer throughly dyen couth' (II. vii. 58). Again and again the poem throws up characters who will not die, who feverishly hold onto bodiless forms of life, clinging to existence despite their shrunken cheeks and withered flesh. Care lingers on in life with 'hollow eyes' (IV. v. 34). Malbecco, transformed into an abstraction by his jealousy, dwells eternally in his cave unable to die: 'Yet can he neuer dye, but dying liues, I And doth himselfe with sorrow new sustaine' (III. x. 60).

This spiritual desiccation is not limited to the enemies of Spenser's poem. It can affect his heroes too, if they succumb – as they often do – to temptations to digress from the chief purpose of their quests. Redcrosse, during his imprisonment by Orgoglio, withers away to nothing: 'and all his vitall powres I Decayd, and all his flesh shronk vp like withered flowres' (I. viii. 41). Characters who are forcibly separated from their ladies also tend to lose their physical substance and fade into hollowness. Timias is so smitten by the loss of Belphoebe's affection 'That like a pined ghost he soon appeares' (IV. vii. 41), and Marinell, separated from his love Florimell, 'Gan fade, and liuely spirits deaded quight: I His cheeke bones raw, and eie-pits hollow grew' (IV. xii. 20). Life in death is the negative side of Spenser's ambition to revive the past. And it can strike anyone in the poem, hero or villain.

Spenser's heroes are almost always associated with the airy and the vital. Whilst they perform the most physical of deeds, their material substance is often thinned by epithets such as 'nimble', or 'light', or by Spenser's favourite adverb, 'lightly'. *The Faerie Queene* has a repertoire of staple phrases (so and so 'leeped lightly from the ground', or 'dismounted light'), which almost always indicate that a character is about deservedly to win a battle. Contact with the heavy matter of earth, however, or with 'fleshly slime', almost always means danger or disgrace, and brings with it flavours of the contaminatingly mortal. Spenser's heroes are poised between spiritualized perfection and the heaviness of the flesh, and often enact battles between the principles of lightness and earth. In his climactic battle with the dragon, Redcrosse – whose name 'George' derives from the Greek word for earth – 'From loathed soile he can him lightly reare' (I. xi. 39): light ascent from the bodily is one aspect of his heroic mission. The word 'ground' in *The Faerie Queene* can be used as a general epithet for the world (as in 'the fayrest mayd on ground' (VII. vii. 34)); but more usually it evokes a state of death or defeat, as when Disdaine 'fell to ground, like to a lumpe of durt' (VI. viii. 16). It is where the vanquished fall, and what they turn into when they have lost the lightness of life and its aspirations towards perfection.

The chief enemy of the House of Alma, and perhaps the most brilliantly portrayed of all Spenser's villains, is Maleger. He is generally regarded as a representation of Original Corruption, which permanently assails the mortal body. But his poetic flavour fits in with the themes explored so far in this chapter. He combines the fleetness of foot which Spenser would expect from his heroes (he rides a Tiger, a 'light-foot beast' (II. xi. 25)) with the deathless deadliness which is the negative version of the poem's own wish to revitalize the past:

> Full large he was of limbe, and shoulders brode,
> But of such subtile substance and vnsound,
> That like a ghost he seem'd, whose graue-clothes were vnbound.
>
> (II. xi. 20)

The first line here promises a substantial adversary, perhaps one of the giant sons of earth who rumble destructively through *The Faerie Queene*, before the giant melts into an insubstantial zombie, alive in death. Maleger is born of the earth, and so revives every time Arthur cuts his dead body to the ground. His mingling of airy substanceless and heavy ties to the soil prompts one of Spenser's finest similes, in which he describes the giant's revival after Arthur's first attempt to kill him:

> As when *Ioues* harnesse-bearing Bird from hie
> Stoupes at a flying heron with proud disdaine,
> The stone-dead quarrey fals so forciblie,
> That it rebounds against the lowly plaine,
> A second fall redoubling back againe.
>
> (II. xi. 43)

'Stone-dead quarrey' magnificently digs its roots into the earth: the stoney weight of that word 'quarrey' pulls the corpse to earth, as it thumps and rebounds in a parody of life. Maleger is a Spenserian revival of a classical myth. He derives from the mythological giant Antaeus, who is repeatedly killed by Hercules, and who repeatedly revives when dropped to the ground, until Hercules realizes that contact with the giant's mother earth is giving his enemy an endless shot of life. The adversaries of Spenser's knights are often creatures who are linked with the earth, either by their biological origins (repeatedly Spenser associates the enemies of his knights with the race of giants, who are born out of the earth), or by their death. Sansfoy 'With bloudy mouth his mother earth did kis' (I. ii. 19) when he dies. Grantorto dies, and 'falling on his mother earth he fed' (V. xii. 23), and is 'lightly' (!) reft of his head by Arthegall. Orgoglio the giant is a child of earth: 'The greatest Earth his vncouth mother was', who generates from a build up of wind 'this monstrous masse of earthly slime' (I. vii. 9). Conquest of the giants is a precondition for the establishment of the British nation, according to both Geoffrey of Monmouth and the chronicle of Britain read by Arthur in II. x. 7–9, and in this context the earthiness of Spenserian adversaries has an edge to it: it suggests that the old, raw earth of England has continually to be reconquered in order to create an empire which will live on. But Maleger also represents a particularly potent kind of earthly villain for Spenser's poem, since he is the twin of the poem's attempt to reanimate the writing of the past. *The Faerie Queene* seeks to revitalize ancient heroic writing; its dynastic heroes seek to perpetuate their blood-line, and make it live for ever, and their vividly imagined adversaries suck their life blood from these drives to eternal life.

Spenser has been seen, notably by C. S. Lewis, as a poet of vitality, whose works offer 'images of life'. Lewis means by this that *The Faerie Queene* contains images of living, sexual vitality, and praises the processes of biological reproduction which give rise to that vitality. *The Faerie Queene* does contain many hermaphrodites, who promise a continuing vitality from their unification of both sexes in one body. The Venus described by Scudamour in the Temple of Venus 'Begets and eke conceiues' (IV. x. 41). In the Temple of Isis (V. vii) Britomart witnesses the fusion of male and female principles through a dream of the union between a lion and a crocodile. The 1590 ending of the three-book poem presents, as we have seen, the image of Scudamour and Amoret fused together like 'that faire *Hermaphrodite*, | Which that rich *Romane* of white marble wrought' (III. xii. 46, 1590 version). Such visions of sexual union provide the poem with suitably endless endings: they appear to resolve divergent elements and separated couples, and at the same time promise a continuation of life. The Mutabilitie Cantos conclude with the most powerful hermaphrodite of all – the figure of Nature:

> Whether she man or woman inly were,
> That could not any creature well descry:
> For, with a veile that wimpled euery where,
> Her head and face was hid, that mote to none appeare.

(VII. vii. 5)

But although Nature, surrounded with burgeoning growth, and warmly accepting of the changeful vitality of the universe, ends the poem as we have it, *The Faerie Queene* is not simply, as Lewis would put it, 'on the side of life'. It is also fascinated by people who lack life. And it is not just fascinated, but also horrified, by the uncontrollable vitality of the natural world. The first image of natural fertility which we encounter in the poem is the monster Errour, whose brood of children feed upon her blood ('Making her death their life' (I. i. 25)), and whose very vomit lives. Errour spews up pamphlets which teem with horrid life, and which introduce one of the most powerful images of naturally self-regenerating power in the whole poem: 'The fertile Nile, which creatures new doth frame' (IV. xi. 20):

> Her vomit full of bookes and papers was,
> With loathly frogs and toades, which eyes did lacke...
>
> .   .   .   .
>
> As when old father *Nilus* gins to swell
> With timely pride aboue the *Aegyptian* vale,
> His fattie waues do fertile slime outwell,
> And ouerflow each plaine and lowly dale.

(I. i. 20–1)

The Faerie Queene evokes two opposed but profoundly interconnected mental worlds. In one there is an immortality driven by a thin, dry, despairingly ghostly spirit, or by the teemingly

67

uncontrollable fecundity of Errour; in the other there is a pressure towards organic perpetuity. These two worlds are stitched together by a web of verbal correspondences so tight as to make them almost indistinguishable. Epic has always thrived on the generation of internal correspondences: Homer often uses the same oral formulae to describe the actions of both the Greeks and the Trojans; Virgil, with conscious artifice, uses similar terms to describe the deaths of both Rome's imperial enemies and those who die for the future of his empire. Spenser's poem goes further in its willingness to associate type and antitype, weaving them into a text which feeds off the dangers implicit in its own ambition to revive the past.

The Garden of Adonis lies at the centre of the six books of *The Faerie Queene*, in III. vi, and it is a central part of the imaginative vision of the poem. The Garden is an atemporal, personless location: it cannot be simply related to the rest of the action of Book III, and, although Amoret is said to be raised there, no knight either elfin or human ever comes within it. The Garden is placed in the most fertile of imaginative locations for Spenser. It occupies an unspecified past, a period of 'antique' perfection which lies behind all history, but which is untouched by human action. The Garden is a realm of change, and of rebirth, presenting a kind of immortality through continual regeneration which is realized nowhere else in the poem. In the main narrative, characters seek each other's love, but never breed; in the Garden, liberated from the constraints of time, and from the fallible emotions of heroes, Spenser explores a form of changefulness which is full of life. The description of the Garden is introduced by a story about the miraculous birth of the twins Belphoebe and Amoret from the union of a sunbeam with a nymph, Chrysogone. This is in part a piece of sanitizing mythology, since at the allegorical level Belphoebe is a type of Elizabeth I, whose actual birth, from the union of Henry VIII and Anne Boleyn, was discoloured by her mother's subsequent execution for adultery. In Spenser's fiction her birth becomes an example of the natural miracle of fertility:

> Miraculous may seeme to him, that reades
> So straunge ensample of conception;
> But reason teacheth that the fruitfull seades
> Of all things liuing, through impression

Of the sunbeames in moyst complexion,
Doe life conceiue and quickned are by kynd:
So after *Nilus* invndation,
Infinite shapes of creatures men do fynd,
Informed in the mud, on which the Sunne hath shynd.

(III. vi. 8)

This describes a moment of perfect sexual fusion, when the sun beats down on and pierces a womb with life. It evokes a kind of love that is purely creative, and which has deliberate overtones of the Virgin Birth. But *The Faerie Queene* so completely entangles its images of good and bad that even the myth of Belphoebe's birth is not without its distracting twins. The image of the Nile invites readers to cast their mind back to the endless spawning of Errour's brood, and fashions a direct and disturbing link between the birth of a Protestant princess and the spawn of Errour, which might make a wary reader recall that Elizabeth I and her Catholic sister Mary shared the same father. Truth and error are never completely separable in the poem: 'truth' can only be defined in opposition to error, and the process of opposing is also a form of comparing.

The description of the Garden of Adonis is also entangled in the verbal texture of the rest of the poem. In particular Spenser's description picks out phrases from the earlier part of Book III, in which Britomart had so hopelessly aspired to a dynastic union with Arthegall, and gives to those phrases a vitality which they did not have when they were used before. The twins Amoret and Belphoebe, 'wondrously were begot and bred'. This phrase harks back to the birth of Merlin, who was 'wondrously begotten' not by a sunbeam, but 'By false illusion of a guilefull Spright I On a faire Ladie Nonne' (III. iii. 13). Even the perfect creativity of the Garden of Adonis resonates darkly with the false births which sprinkle the rest of the poem. The Garden does not offer a simple escape from the duplicities of making, or from the sorrow which attends upon all efforts to revive a dead past. At its centre is the figure of Adonis, who is Spenser's greatest image of death in life and life in death. Gored by a boar, the boy is rescued and continually revived by Venus, the goddess of love:

There wont faire *Venus* often to enioy
Her deare *Adonis* ioyous company,
And reape sweet pleasure of the wanton boy;

> There yet, some say, in secret he does ly,
> Lapped in flowres and pretious spycery,
> By her hid from the world, and from the skill
> Of *Stygian* Gods, which doe her loue enuy;
> But she her selfe, when euer that she will,
> Possesseth him, and of his sweetnesse takes her fill.
>
> And sooth it seemes they say: for he may not
> For euer die, and euer buried bee
> In balefull night, where all things are forgot;
> All be he subiect to mortalitie,
> Yet is eterne in mutabilitie,
> And by succession made perpetuall,
> Transformed oft, and chaunged diuerselie:
> For him the Father of all formes they call:
> Therefore needs mote he liue, that liuing giues to all.
>
> (III. vi. 46–7)

These stanzas evoke a timeless world of endless regeneration, with a fragile Spenserian awareness that the world they describe may not even definitely exist ('And sooth *it seemes* they say'). 'There wont' intimates that Venus both once did, and now does, and will reap sweet pleasures of her paramour. The vision of Adonis is the central example of the wish of Spenser's poem to make the past live on. But again its perfection is qualified by echoes of what has come before. Adonis has more than a trace of the despairingly endless incapacity to die of Despaire, who tries to kill himself: 'But death he could not worke himselfe thereby; I For thousand times he so himselfe had drest, I Yet nathelesse it could not doe him die I Till he should die his last, that is eternally' (I. ix. 54). He anticipates the deathless progression towards no death which is Malbecco ('Yet can he neuer dye, but dying liues' (III. x. 60)). And he also harkens back to the moment when Britomart's nurse, Glauce, is urging her – with the unscrupulousness which literary nurses have had ever since Euripides' *Hippolytus* – to follow her desires and to breed. 'And euer buried bee I In baleful night' re-echoes the nurse's exhortation to her charge not to be coy, and so

>   lose
> Both leafe and fruit, both too vntimely shed,
> As one in wilfull bale for euer buried.
>
> (III. ii. 31)

The perpetual vitality of Adonis is the closest we get to the fertile, dynastic ending which the poem, and Glauce, promise for Britomart: she never marries her Arthegall, and her story is only fulfilled by this hopeful echo which links her tale with one of endless death and rebirth. But the figure of Adonis also casts a melancholy light on the wishful thinking which underlies the whole poem. He is 'by *succession* made perpetual'. In 1590, as the Queen aged and remained unmarried, the ideal of perpetual succession – in the literal, political, sense – was unattainable. Elizabeth would die, and many feared in the 1590s that Protestant England would die with her. Although Adonis is the only promise of a future completion of the dynastic project of *The Faerie Queene*, even his world is fragile. 'Wicked *Time*' intrudes into the ideal repose of Adonis, pitilessly destroying the flowers and fruits of the Garden:

> He flyes about, and with his flaggy wings
> Beates downe both leaues and buds without regard,
> Ne euer pittie may relent his malice hard.

(III. vi. 39)

Spenser loves fragility. He is not a poet of life so much as a poet of mortality, for whom the energies of living and the forces of frailty exert an equal and interlinking charm. He needs to have a force within the Garden rendering it fragile before it can completely ignite his imagination. And that figure of Time, pitilessly destroying the perfection of the Garden, uncannily recalls the violent actions of Guyon as he destroyed the Bowre of Blisse with 'rigour pittilesse'. Spenser cannot forget about his fallible mortal heroes, even when he is attempting to imagine perfection. Even Adonis – who has some claim to be the one true dynastic hero of the poem, the one hero who endlessly breeds, and endlessly revives – reflects images of what is good in the poem, and refracts images of what is bad.

6

Wild Men and Wild Places

The Faerie Queene contains a further band of characters who occupy the hinterland between the good and the bad. These might be called its sylvan characters. The poem is full of creatures who grow from the woods, and who have the unpredictable energy of the natural. A group of satyrs rescues Una from Sansloy in I. vi, and then falls down before her in idolatrous worship. A 'saluage nation' in VI. viii captures Serena, ties her up, and salivates hungrily over her lily flesh. In Book IV Arthegall, disguised as a salvage knight, bedecked with branches, wins the Tournament of Florimell's girdle. Wood-gods and wildmen have a long history as figures on the boundaries of civility, whose moral nature might either be subhuman, or a perfect antitype to the contaminating civility of courts.[1] In the 1590s such figures had a particular energy. Puttenham gives a peculiar priority to satyrs and woody figures in his brief history of poetic genres, attributing to them the origins of satire, in which it is 'as if the gods of the woods, whom they called *Satyres* or *Silvanes*, should appear and recite those verses of rebuke'.[2] Foresters and forest dwellers also play a powerful role in courtly entertainments of the 1570s and 1580s, in the period when Spenser was first planning his epic, and such creatures, emerging from bushes or brakes in entertainments put on by the Earl of Leicester, frequently do so to admonish or advise the Queen. *The Faerie Queene* feeds off the equivocal and admonitory powers of such beings. In I. vi, after Una is worshipped by the satyrs, Sir Satyrane appears. Born of a passionate woodland rape of a 'Lady myld' by a satyr, and 'noursled vp in life and manners wilde' (I. vi. 23), his genealogy makes him look more likely to assault than to rescue Una. But 'wilde' for Spenser is not a synonym for 'bad': the sylvan figure of Sir Satyrane, poised on the uncertain boundary between the wild and the civil, rescues the heroine, and 'learnd her discipline of faith and veritie' (I. vi. 31).

The second instalment of *The Faerie Queene*, published in 1596, in general gives far more weight to the wild and the sylvan than the first three books. It is also far more sceptical in its treatment of heroes. Arthur and Arthegall in Book V frequently adopt stratagems in order to defeat the enemies of justice: they disguise themselves in the armour of knights whom they have killed (V. viii. 25), and use a damsel as bait to lure the guileful Malengin from his lair (V. ix. 8). Calidore in Book VI is quite capable of a gracious lie to save the honour of a lady, and spends the majority of his book in quiet retreat from the active life, contemplating the charms of his mistress in pastoral seclusion. He also has an edge of guile: before attempting to rescue Pastorella 'him armed priuily' beneath his shepherd's clothes (VI. xi. 36). Calepine shares his wiles: he hides behind Serena at one point to avoid Sir Turpine's sword (VI. iii. 49). These emergent features of Spenser's heroes in all probability reflect major shifts in European political thought at the close of the sixteenth century. For early humanists, such as Erasmus (1466–1536), there is a straightforward relation between virtue and participation in government: the virtuous ideally either rule, or counsel a monarch how to rule virtuously. A similar political vision is outlined by Spenser's friend Ludovic Bryskett in his *Discourse of Civill Life* (1606), the prologue to which contains what is presented as a speech by Spenser himself to the effect that he had explored the relations between government and virtue in *The Faerie Queene*. This correlation of virtue and civic activity has a strong influence on the allegorical design of the first instalment of the poem, in which knights at once explore what virtue is and put that virtue to the service of Gloriana their Queen. In the early 1590s, however, particularly in the circles of Sir Walter Ralegh and the Earl of Essex, there are signs of an emergent 'new humanism', which had its roots in the uneasy political environments of France and Italy. This form of humanism, associated with thinkers such as Botero, Lipsius, and Montaigne, presented a less simple view of the relations between virtue and government. Good citizens, in the manner of classical stoics, would retreat from active participation in the state and concentrate instead on controlling their own passions. A further strand of this tradition emphasized what became known as 'ragion di stato' (reason of state), according to which the criterion by which actions should be judged was not their absolute virtue but their effectiveness in contributing to the just running of the commonwealth.[3] Spenser may well have been responding to these currents of thought when he fashioned the withdrawal of Calidore from the active life, and when he presented Arthegall and Arthur guilefully defeating the guileful.

But Book VI, 'Contayning the Legend of S. Calidore. Or of Courtesie', also shows much deeper signs that the cultural mission of fashioning a gentleman, which the poem originally undertook, is wandering off course, and that Spenser's own experience of life in Ireland is shifting the centre of the poem away from the courtly. These signs are written deep into the imagery and environment of the book. Book VI belongs to the last phase of *The Faerie Queene*, which turns away from the court and the demands of active civic participation, and which seeks to find a new seat of virtue which is 'deepe within the mynd' (VI. pr. 5). This new urge for privacy is reflected in Calidore's remark that 'in each mans self ... | It is, to fashion his owne lyfes estate' (VI. ix. 31): rather than seeking to 'fashion' a gentleman, Calidore seeks merely to fashion his own life. His quest is to 'track' (that is, to pursue, rather than finally to kill) the Blattant Beast – and the verb, suggestive of woody pursuits (*OED*, sense 3a of 'quest': 'The search for game made by hounds'), reveals a lot about the environment of Book VI. The Beast chiefly lurks in woods, and emerges whenever women or men could be thought to be behaving badly: it has no final dwelling (and most of the monsters in *The Faerie Queene* 'dwell', often in rocky and barren locations), and is never killed, since it represents a body of adversaries, slander and discourtesy, which are unkillable. The hero of Book VI is engaged in a battle which he simply cannot win, and he is caught in a landscape which is increasingly resistant to his attempts to fashion it. The centre of Book VI lies, not in courts and civilization, but in woods and wild places. A salvage man of unknown parentage, who lives and grows in the forest, repeatedly comes to the rescue of those who are beset by uncivil knights. The naturally noble Tristram, who dwells 'amongst the woodie Gods' (VI. ii. 26), also assists the failing hero. A hermit, dwelling in a woody chapel 'all with Yuy ouerspred' (VI. v. 35), manages to cure the wounds inflicted by the Blattant Beast as the book's hero cannot; and a herb growing in 'the thickest wood' can staunch bleeding (VI. iv. 12), where the powers of courtesy fail.

All of these bosky features are standard elements in prose romances, but in their context within *The Faerie Queene* and within Spenser's life they take on extremely strong resonances. Book VI is one of the latest instalments of Spenser's gradual imaginative devolution from the court. In *Colin Clouts Come Home Againe*, which was printed the year before Book VI in 1595, Colin returns home to Ireland to deplore the excesses of the English court, becoming a poet who sings of the corruption of the centre from a wild margin of the nation. In the later 1590s Spenser was becoming a writer whose interests, as an expatriate English planter in Ireland, who paid rent to the Crown for an estate of 3,000 acres, drew him away from the quest for Gloriana and into the wilds. Digging, weeding, and cultivation were all key metaphors in the vocabulary of the New English in Ireland when they described the process of extirpating the native stock of the country, and of 'cultivating' the land. These associations run very deep in Western culture – the very word 'culture', like 'cultivation', derives from the Latin word for digging, and the word 'colony' from *colonus*, or 'farmer'. The inability of 'culture' finally to affect the wild energies of the land in Book VI marks a crisis in the poem: Spenser is beginning uncertainly to realize that the process of cultivation which he is attempting may not have the strength to transform the rude, sylvan energies of the landscape. The physical, and increasingly the metaphorical, environment of Book VI is rawly untameable, and resists the cultural energies of civility. The salvage nation which captures Serena does not use 'the painefull plough' (VI. viii. 35), and the benevolent salvage man 'neither plough'd nor sowed' (VI. iv. 14). The book also contains many similes drawn from the woodland sport of hawking (VI. iv. 19), and its heroes have a trace of the wild: Calepine is compared to a 'wilde goate' at VI. iii. 49. Similes drawn from the processes of agriculture in Book VI do not triumphally explore the power of man to conquer the land, but usually evoke a vain struggle with the untameable. When the uncivil Scorn tries to bind Sir Enias, his efforts are compared to the strife of a 'sturdy ploughman' to force a steer 'the buxome yoke to beare' (VI. viii. 12). And in that tiny episode it is worth noting that the wish to cultivate is felt by what should be the villains of the episode. By 1596 Spenser has instinctively ceased to see the process of cultivation as a heroic one.

Book VI is also laced with the language of the school. The verb 'to learn' occurs in it more often than in any other book, and several figures within it have names which have odd associations with great humanist educators. Sir Aldine's name recalls in anglicized form that of Aldus Manutius, the first and greatest Venetian humanist printer; Sir Calepine's name might remind many an ex-schoolboy of Calepinus, the composer of a major Renaissance dictionary. But the book's interest in the educative never quite meshes creatively with the wild energies it releases: it is very thinly populated with characters, like Satyrane in the more optimistic world of Book I, who actually learn. The salvage man has a native ability to express rage or compassion 'By speaking signes' (VI. v. 4), and can produce a 'soft murmure, and confused sound I Of senselesse words, which nature did him teach' (VI. iv. 11), but he never learns a human language. At the climax of the book Sir Calidore, in his rural retreat from heroic activity, intrudes on a vision of the Graces dancing around the poet Colin Clout. Colin's piping is set against a sylvan backdrop ('It was an hill plaste in an open plaine, I That round about was bordered with a wood' (VI. x. 6)) which is filled with Spenser's characteristic echoing song ('That through the woods their Eccho did rebound' (VI. x. 10)). Calidore, though, lurks in the privy margin of the wood, and is more interested in leering than in learning.

> But in the couert of the wood did byde,
> Beholding all, yet of them vnespyde.
> There he did see, that pleased much his sight,
> That euen he him selfe his eyes enuyde,
> An hundred naked maidens lilly white,
> All raunged in a ring, and daunsing in delight.

> (VI. x. 11)

As Calidore nosily emerges from his hiding place to inspect the naked maidens more closely, the Graces vanish from his intrusive gaze, and the poet Colin Clout breaks his pipe in despair. Calidore does not simply seek spiritual discipline from the vision, but – like an intrusive courtly interpreter of *The Faerie Queene* – asks the poet to explain his vision. Colin dutifully sets about translating his private sylvan communion into a form which might educate a courtly knight:

These three on men all gracious gifts bestow,
Which decke the body or adorne the mynde,
To make them louely or well fauoured show,
As comely carriage, entertainement kynde,
Sweete semblaunt, friendly offices that bynde,
And all the complements of curtesie:
They teach vs, how to each degree and kynde
We should our selues demeane, to low, to hie;
To friends, to foes, which skill men call Ciuility.

(VI. x. 23)

Colin's rudely didactic ('They teach vs') allegorical gloss on his secret vision is close in its phrasing to the entry for 'the Graces' in the most frequently used English–Latin dictionary in the sixteenth century, that of Thomas Cooper. He is perhaps deliberately trying to sound more like a schoolmaster than a poet. The apparatus of bookish learning impedes the visionary in Book VI: and it is hard to see that Calidore himself has drunk instruction from the vision into which he has intruded. The weight of the poem has shifted away from learned heroism and towards the land, towards the visionary spaces of woods and their native energies. The poet himself has become a creature of the wilds, aware that his vision will never coincide with the realities of courtliness.

It is in the Mutabilitie Cantos, those evocative final fragments of the poem, which are very likely to have been the last passages to have been composed, that this growing sympathy with the land comes to a head. In them Spenser sets aside the frailty of mortal heroes altogether, and turns his eye instead to the natural energies of the wilds. Nature is summoned to Arlo Hill in Ireland to judge Mutabilitie's claim that she rules the universe. In a sardonic echo of his earlier question 'who knowes not *Colin Clout*?' (VI. x. 16), Spenser asks 'Who knowes not *Arlo Hill*?' (VII. vi. 36). Readers in England would be very unlikely to have heard of Arlo; but inhabitants of Ireland would know of it for sure, since it was a notorious hide-out for Irish robbers and rebels. Before Nature is introduced to judge the case, Spenser indulges in a sportive digression about the prehistory of Arlo, in which sylvan characters come to dominate the foreground of his poem, and in which his writing takes on some of the satirical flavour with which Puttenham associated woodland creatures. The satyr Faunus wants to see the goddess Diana naked, and so suborns Molanna, a

77

stream in which the virgin goddess bathes, to let him spy on her. In punishment Diana does not kill Faunus (since he, a creature of the land, like Adonis, 'must for euer liue' (VII. vi. 50)); instead she abandons and violates the whole landscape:

> Nath'lesse, *Diana*, full of indignation,
>   Thence-forth abandond her delicious brooke;
>
>   .   .   .   .
>
>   And all that Mountaine, which doth over-looke
>   The richest champian that may else be rid,
> And the faire *Shure*, in which are thousand Salmons bred.
>
> Them all, and all that she so deare did way,
>   Thence-forth she left; and parting from the place,
>   There-on an heauy haplesse curse did lay,
>   To weet, that Wolues, where she was wont to space,
>   Should harbour'd be, and all those Woods deface,
>   And Thieues should rob and spoile that Coast around.
>   Since which, those Woods, and all that goodly Chase,
>   Doth to this day with Wolues and Thieues abound:
> Which too-too true that lands in-dwellers since haue found.
>
>   (VII. vi. 54–5)

Spenser is often now regarded as primarily a poet of empire, whose role as an administrator in Ireland permeates the whole of *The Faerie Queene* with colonial violence. The Mutabilitie Cantos were probably written at around the same time as, or possibly after, the *Vewe of the Present State of Ireland* (1596), Spenser's critique of Elizabethan policy in Ireland. It is tempting to make connections between the two works; but a simple equation does not quite work. In the Mutabilitie Cantos it is the *active* destructiveness of Diana that mars Arlo Hill, whereas, in Spenser's *Vewe*, it was the passivity of his Queen's foreign policy which was endangering the subjugation of Ireland. In the *Vewe* it is *imperfect* colonization that creates legal and social problems in Ireland, whereas in the Mutabilitie Cantos the suggestion is that the morally neutral, sylvan forces of the Irish landscape would live on quite happily without any interference from divine or English forces, from either Diana or the Virgin Queen. In the stanza just quoted the virgin goddess is reduced to a spiteful vandal of the land, whose venom can none the less not completely destroy the pulse of vitality, the benignly changeful forces of growth, which run through the Irish landscape. Molanna is given her reward by Faunus, and marries her Fanchin, despite Diana. There is perhaps a colonist's appropriating glint in the eye as Spenser praises the salmon-breeding streams of Arlo Hill (in the *Vewe* he writes 'And sure it is, it is a most bewtifull and swete countrie as anye is under heaven, seamed thoroughe out with manye goodlye rivers replenished with all sortes of fish' (ll. 559–62)); but there is also something more than colonial exploitation at work in the episode: there is a colonist's sense of the uncontrollable energies of the land which he inhabits, and of the vital powers from which he harvests his living. The Mutabilitie Cantos mark the triumph of the sylvan in Spenser's poem: the energies of the land, pulsing vitally on for ever, triumph over the efforts of mortals to control them, and triumph too over empire. When Spenser's weary muse comes to rest at the end of Book VI, ceasing her efforts to cultivate the land and to fashion gentlemen from the rude clay of his readers, we can feel both the despair of a colonial administrator who felt his 'planting' would never change the land, and the delight of a poet for whom the endless power of the earth to continue its life through death was the strongest force in the universe.

7

Love and Empire

Recent criticism of *The Faerie Queene* has been preoccupied with two major issues: the poem's politics and its sexual politics. Both of these areas have generated problems for a modern liberal readership. The poem is often seen as a work which luxuriates in imperialism, and which celebrates the absolute authority of its Queen. It is also often seen as a poem which is founded on the dominance of the male, and which treats women with a 'suspicion' of a kind which should make its readers suspicious.[1] On the face of it, these would seem to be indisputable features of the work. Its heroes spend much of their time conquering and destroying in a way that seems straighforwardly to indicate that they are attempting to expand the empire of Gloriana. Women, and particularly the lower parts of female bodies, are frequently associated with deception: Errour ends in snakey vileness (I. i. 14), and Duessa's guileful beauty is eventually shown to mask hideous nether deformity (I. ii. 41). At many points in the poem women are captured, and at some they are tortured, by men. Florimell spends most of the poem running away from potential captors: she escapes from the lusts of the witch's son only to fall into the hands of a libidinous fisherman, from whom she is rescued by Proteus, who, in turn, imprisons her. Her incarceration continues for more than a whole book, from III. viii to IV. xii. There are times, too, when the poem itself focuses a rapacious and imprisoning eye on its female characters. Its allegorical method often centres a complex array of qualities on a single person, and when these people are women its allegorical eye can become predatory and destructive. Amoret is plucked from a circle of virtues in the Temple of Venus by her husband-to-be Sir Scudamour, and is later discovered by Britomart imprisoned in the Castle of Busirane, forced daily to parade out in an allegorical

80

masque of the God Cupid. After a string of personifications who represent the terrors of love, Amoret, just before the climactic centre of the masque, enters with her naked breast 'Entrenched deepe with knife accursed keene' (III. xii. 20). Serena is placed in an even less invitingly central position when she is seen surrounded by cannibals whose hungry eyes anatomize what they long to bite. 'Her yuorie necke, her alablaster brest' (VI. viii. 42) are described as lovingly as items on a menu.

There are two preliminary points which should be made about these elements of the poem. The first is that fictional representation is not the same thing as advocacy: to represent a group of salacious cannibals salivating over a woman may tempt a reader into collusion with their voracious delight, but it does not recommend their incivility as a norm. Secondly, there is little point in simply reprimanding works from the past. Spenser lived in an age when the majority of women were denied education, and in which many women were married off with very little concern for their wishes. These facts are not his fault. A literary work can, of course, participate in disseminating unjust forms of behaviour by representing them as an unavoidable norm, and so, if one were inclined to rebuke the past for failing to be as enlightened as the present, could warrant some blame. Several recent critics have overcome their desire to criticize *The Faerie Queene* for not being an enlightened twentieth-century work by saying that it 'problematizes' or 'exposes the contradictions which lie within' imperialism, or within a form of sexuality which puts men on top.[2] By this means critics can argue that, although the poem is implicated in all sorts of ideological areas which they do not like, they can still bear to read it because it treats those areas in a way which allows readers to see the arbitrariness or fragility of those ways of thinking.

There is, though, a more radical approach to these aspects of the poem, which is to ask whether the poem's ideal sexual politics *are* actually centred on male dominance, and whether the poem is simply 'imperialist'. Much of this book so far has argued that Spenser was not simply orthodox in his vision of Elizabethan England, and that he was aware of the mortal limits which qualify his own authority, and which restrict his own control over the shape of his poem. He is, I have suggested, a poet whose work is subject both to a literally expressed and to a structurally implicit

81

form of humility: in the final stanzas of the Mutabilitie Cantos, he subjects himself and his authority to higher powers; and in *The Faerie Queene* as a whole he never quite achieves the narrative goals which he sets himself. The Envoy to *The Shepheardes Calender* presents the poem as treading humbly in the footsteps of Chaucer ('Dare not to match thy pype with Tityrus hys style'). This posture of submission suits well with the final vision of Colin Clout in 'December' as a poet who is subjected to seasonal changes and to time. Spenser's ingrained sense of the limitations of human capacities makes it unlikely that he would be a simple advocate of imperious control, since to claim that one force or person should have unqualified control over another force or person would be to assume that people have an unqualified power to realize their desires. This chapter will suggest that characters in *The Faerie Queene* do not simply conquer or dominate their lovers, or the world through which they quest. I shall suggest rather that Spenser is drawn towards a view of love which emphasizes mutuality and consent, and towards a very complex and qualified view of imperial authority. Neither of these areas, as we shall see, is without its attendant problems.

The sexual politics of the poem are not simply rooted in the dominance of the male. Although many characters strive to capture, command, or rape the objects of their desire, they seldom actually succeed in doing so. Spenser's women often flutter away from their male pursuers: their hair is glimpsed flashing through a forest, or flowing out behind them as they gallop fearfully away on their palfreys. Florimell spends much of the poem in flight, and is never finally subjected to any male will. In an odd way Spenser's women are free in flight, in that through flight they enter a realm in which they are not forced into allegorical tableaux or compelled to yield to a man. This sounds like a piece of special pleading of a rather thin sort: it is not much of a defence of a poet who represents women continually on the brink of being raped to say he gives them legs to run away. But the freedom of Spenser's fleeing women to run off into the untamed spaces of the forest is a crucial part of the sexual vision of the poem. *The Faerie Queene* is convinced at a deep, structural level that human designs and desires will fall short of achievement, and the narrative corollary of this is that its would-be rapists almost invariably fail to attain their desires. Many of the most dangerous moments for women in

The Faerie Queene take place in woods or wild places, and often some element from the pulsing background of plural actions of which the poem is made emerges at the last minute to salvage a woman who seems to be about to become a victim of male desires. Proteus' 'rescue' of Florimell is a strong though equivocal example of this: he is an embodiment of slippery mutability, of the raw potentialities which skirt and shape Spenser's universe. He is ungraspably changeful, shifting from a Faerie Knight, to a Giant, to a Centaur, in order to terrify Florimell into submission (III. viii. 39–41). But, because of his intervention, Florimell's fisherman captor is unable to have his way with her; and Proteus himself tries to urge her to consent rather than simply ravishing her. Serena is similarly saved by Calepine, who is 'by chaunce, more then by choyce' (VI. viii. 46) drawn into the woods at the right time to rescue her from being eaten by the cannibals. The Spenserian universe has a sylvan power, and a multiplicity of strands, which together, by chance, or by a more directed 'fortune', stand up for virgins. Would-be dominant men tend to have their plots abruptly (to use Spenser's own word) amputated, just as they near consummation.

The poem's explicit statements about what makes an ideal relationship between the sexes reinforce these features of its structure. Love in *The Faerie Queene* is ideally directed towards a virtuous man or woman, in a manner which has strong Platonic overtones. It is also ideally founded upon the consent of both parties. In this respect Spenser is an heir to a humanist tradition of debates about the nature of marriage, in which a woman has free choice of whom to marry, and reaches her decision by valuing virtue over blood and breeding. In Henry Medwall's play *Fulgens and Lucrece* (c.1496), the first English example of debates of this kind, Lucrece is finally given liberty to choose whom she will marry. Spenser's emphasis on consent in love also develops a theme which plays a central part in Chaucer's *Canterbury Tales*. At the start of Book III Britomart quotes a version of a couplet from *The Franklin's Tale*:

> Ne may loue be compeld by maisterie;
> For soone as maisterie comes, sweet loue anone
> Taketh his nimble wings, and soone away is gone.

> (III. i. 25)

The lines to which Britomart alludes ('Love wol nat been constreyned by maistrye. I Whan maistrie comth, the God of Love anon I Beteth his wynges, and farewel, he is gon!' (ll. 764–6)) are part of Chaucer's extended analysis of how love, being by its nature alien to constraint, and yet being by its nature founded upon a relationship of two people, is bound unsettlingly at once to raise and to seek to overgo the awkward question of who is in control of a relationship.[3] Britomart's version of Chaucer's lines presents love as a 'nimble' thing, which can flit away, as Florimell and Amoret both do, when it is threatened with constraint, and resort to the final freedom of flight.

Spenser, though, despite being drawn to an ideally voluntary love, finds it extremely difficult to represent the moment of consent which issues in the free mutual yielding of lovers. The 1595 volume of *Amoretti and Epithalamion*, which appeared after the first and before the second instalment of *The Faerie Queene*, belongs to a period when Spenser was thinking seriously about marriage, as he contemplated his own union to Elizabeth Boyle. The sonnets attempt to manœuvre the resistant vocabulary of the Petrarchan sonnet, riven with Cupid's tyranny and the stoney dominance of an icy mistress, into expressing a form of love founded on consent. Words which express dominance are woven in and out of the early part of the *Amoretti*: 'thrall', 'captive', 'siege', 'conquer', and 'triumph' all ring through the sequence, as the desperate lover lays siege to his lady's heart, and she, a tyrannical mistress on the Petrarchan model, refuses to yield. The only prospect of a love free of maisterie comes from the hope that the roles of the two lovers will eventually be reversed:

> See how the Tyrannesse doth joy to see
> the huge massacres which her eyes do make:
>
> .   .   .   .
> But her proud hart doe thow a little shake
>
> .   .   .   .
> That I may laugh at her in equall sort,
> as she doth laugh at me and makes my pain her sport.
>
> (Sonnet 10)

The word 'equall' here offers no more than the prospect of alternate superiority in which the thrall will become the conqueror, and the mocker the mocked. The sequence does soften, however, and moves towards a less strifeful form of _equality._ In Sonnet 57 the lovers declare a truce; in 64 they kiss; and by 65 the bands of love have become liberating:

> Sweet be the bands, the which true love doth tye,
> without constraynt or dread of any ill:
> the gentle bird feeles no captivity
> within her cage, but singes and feeds her fill.

(Sonnet 65)

Alastair Fowler, in the previous volume on Spenser in this series, remarked that 'there is a tenderness and a reciprocity of feeling here that would be impossible to match anywhere else in the Renaissance sonnet'.[4] One might, though, sceptically note that the lady is still in a cage, for all her singing. The metaphors of binding and control prove impossible entirely to disentangle from the language of love in the _Amoretti_. The lady remains her lover's prey even when she is yielding to him voluntarily: indeed her own free decision to be bound to her lover eventually imprisons herself: 'till I in hand her yet halfe trembling tooke, I and _with her owne goodwill_ hir fyrmely tyde' (Sonnet 67). Freely she may have agreed, but she still ends up tied like a trembling sparrow to its captor. For all Spenser's efforts to make the _Amoretti_ explore love without maisterie, their language resists.

The _Fowre Hymes_ of 1596 display a similarly fitful argument of love, beginning in an environment of subjection, and attempting to end in a relationship of mutual humility. The 'Hymne in Honour of Love' lauds the power of the 'imperious boy' (l. 120) Cupid, while the lover struggles to perform the 'puissant conquest' (l. 221) which might win the grace of his mistress. 'An Hymne in Honour of Beautie' moves hesitantly towards a love founded upon 'a celestiall harmonie, I Of likely harts composd of starres concent, I Which joyne together in sweete sympathie' (ll. 197–9). That word 'concent' has a flicker of its homophone 'consent'; but its primary sense suggests instinctive and involuntary harmony rather than willing union. A love based on voluntary accord is the ideal towards which the _Hymnes_ tend; but it is an ideal which is given a chance to live only when Spenser turns from earthly love and beauty, which concern the first two _Hymnes_, to heavenly beauty and heavenly love, which are the subjects of the last. The preface to the _Hymnes_ presents the later poems as palinodes which seek to cancel and transcend the youthful amorousness of the first two, which, Spenser claims, had been disseminated abroad by the circulation of manuscript copies. No manuscript copies of the poems survive, however, and it is likely that Spenser's epistle is a fiction designed to suggest to a popular readership that the *Fowre Hymnes* were well liked in courtly circles. The later poems advance the same argument of love, hesitantly progressing out of the language of contention in the first two, onwards towards a love which is divine. The 'Hymne of Heavenly Love' presents the voluntary sacrifice of Christ for man, and the free submission by mankind to Christ out of gratitude for his sacrifice, as the perfect instance of love. It is founded on mutual yielding, rather than on conquest or domination. Christ voluntarily subjected himself to take on a human form; and his love should be answered by a similarly voluntary decision to love and to obey: 'And give thy selfe unto him full and free, | That full and freely gave himself to thee' (ll. 265–6). An ideal love is a gift that is mutually free.

The 1596 instalment of *The Faerie Queene* explores the relations between love and freedom with a similar intentness, and encounters dilemmas similar to those found in the *Amoretti*. When, in Book IV, the Thames woos the Medway, his long efforts to persuade his love to mingle with his waters end with the gracious yielding of his recalcitrant mistress:

> Long had the *Thames* (as we in records reed)
> Before that day her wooed to his bed;
> But the proud Nymph would for no wordly meed,
> Nor no entreatie to his loue be led;
> Till now at last relenting, she to him was wed.

> (IV. xi. 8)

The marriage which results has its origins in the Medway's consent; but Spenser gallops through the processes by which she came to yield to her lover's entreaties with disturbing haste. It takes only five syllables to move from 'relenting' to the marriage. Although he is attracted to the ideal of a consenting union at the theoretical level, he is unable to represent it in practice. In the *Epithalamion*, as we have seen in Chapter 2, the ceremonial description of the wedding swamps the moment when the lady gives her consent to the union ('Why blush ye love to give to me your hand, | The pledge of all our band?' (ll. 238–9)); and in *The*

86

Faerie Queene the catalogue of the rivers of England and Ireland which follows the Medway's yielding similarly drowns out that crucial moment when the Kentish river chooses to become one with the Londony Thames. Her will is subordinated to a Spenserian tableau of images. And while her wedding is occurring, offstage Florimell is languishing in prison, captured by Proteus and held in his watery prison, as a reminder that maisterie can never entirely be eradicated from love.

Spenser's sense of our, and of his own, frailty is so great that the whole of his poem is a sweet fugitive: it presents us with an ideal, which is always almost being realized, but which then just slips tantalizingly through our fingers the moment it appears to be about to come into our hands. *The Faerie Queene* has ambitions and aspirations which it cannot always realize, and the poem continually gives its readers the impression that they are on the quest for an ideal, which, like the Faerie Queene herself, is always two steps ahead, behind, or beyond them. The ideal of love without maisterie is the greatest of the poem's unrealizable goals. It is only through brief epiphanies – through images of hermaphroditic union of the sexes, or momentary visions of asexual reproduction such as those presented in the Garden of Adonis – that Spenser comes close to representing love without maisterie. At these moments Spenser is attempting the greatest and hardest task which fiction can perform: he is using a narrative or mythic structure to evoke an ideal which is not simply formulable in the language which he received. But in the sections of the poem which concern mortal and elfin characters no one actually enacts the elusive ideal of a perfectly mutual union of lovers, because, perhaps, a love that was *completely* without any element of constraint would not be recognizable by mortals as the frustrating, unequal, alternatingly domineering thing which experience, and Spenser's received language, shows love to be. Repeatedly, though, Spenser emphasizes the connectedness of love and consent, with a will to grant his ladies the freedom to choose a mate and to resist an aggressor. After the tournament of Florimell's girdle, Satyrane, the woody knight who rescues Una from the Satyrs, insists that the False Florimell be allowed freely to decide whose lady she should become, once Britomart, the victor at the tourney, has declined to be her lord: 'Sweete is the loue that comes alone with willingnesse' (IV. v. 25), he says. The False

Florimell goes on to make a free choice; and she chooses the false knight Braggadocchio as her lord. The freedom of her choice does not make it a rational one. Nor is the False Florimell's choice likely to ensure for her a life without maisterie, since Braggadocchio had earlier attempted to violate the chaste Belphoebe (II. iii. 42) with an aggressive assault. The poem continually presents alternate versions of its own ideals; and the ideal of love without maisterie is one which it figures forth in various distorted forms. Britomart's lines on the dangers of maisterie in love are later turned into justification of libertinage by Duessa: 'For Loue is free, and led with selfe delight, I Ne will enforced be with maisterdome or might' (IV. i. 46). Britomart's chaste epigram is parodied in order to sanction endless changefulness and infidelity. Scudamour's description of how he took Amoret from the Temple of Venus too is riven with maisterie: 'She often prayd, and often me besought, I Sometime with tender teares to let her goe' (IV. x. 57). The subsequent history of their affair reflects its rough beginnings: Amoret's imprisonment by Busirane, and her subjection to her suffering role in the masque of Cupid, has its origins in, and is an allegorical development of, the initial maisterie of her lover. It is not Spenser's ideal: it is an image of violently defective love which composes part of a complex allegorical exploration of how love might be freed from dominance.

Spenser is not only fighting his language in his efforts to represent love without maisterie. He is also fighting some of the most potent areas of his culture. He lived in a period when love was woven into the texture of political authority. Elizabeth I was well able to use the sweet constraints of love to win her courtiers' obedience to her magisterial will. Her godson, Sir John Harington, the translator of Ariosto, recorded that:

> Her speech did winne all affections, and hir subjectes did try to shewe all love to hir commandes; for she woude say, 'hir state did require her to commande, what she knew hir people woude willingely do from their owne love to hir'. Herein did she shewe hir wysdome fullie: for who did chuse to lose hir confidence; or who woude wythholde a shewe of love and obedience, when their Sovereign said it was their own choice, and not hir compulsion?[5]

Under a monarch who so adroitly could use the supposed freedom of love to bully an apparently free obedience from her subjects, Spenser was all but bound to fail in his attempt to represent a form of love which was free from the contaminating influence of power. But he is also prevented from realizing the ideal for which he strives by his own medium. Spenser's main way of exploring the nature of love is through representations of knightly conquest. A woman might be won from her existing lord by a knight who has defeated him in battle, and she might feel bound to her rescuer as a result – Serena is rescued by the salvage man in VI. v. 9, and seems to be more 'the conquest of his might, I Gotten by spoyle, then purchaced aright'; and Amoret is rescued from 'deadly thraldome' in Busirane's castle by Britomart, and feels obliged to her rescuer, 'Yet dread of shame, and doubt of fowle dishonor I Made her not yeeld so much, as due she deemed' (IV. i. 8). In these circumstances the relationship between knight and lady is evidently not free, but is steeped in the obligations born of conquest and constraint.

The fictional types which the poem uses to describe love are continually fighting – often literally fighting – against its ambition to rid love of maisterie. When Britomart finally encounters her future partner Arthegall, the two fight as equally matched adversaries, with maisterie swaying between them (both are 'Sometimes pursewing, and sometimes pursewed' (IV. vi. 18)). Arthegall eventually 'chaunct' to slice away Britomart's visor, and

> With that her angels face, vnseene afore,
> Like to the ruddie morne appeard in sight.

(IV. vi. 19)

Arthegall attempts to continue fighting, but finds his sword droops in his hand at the wonder of her face. He then finds himself falling to his knees in worship: his victory does not issue in conquest, but in an instinctive self-subjection. In the truce which follows, the lovers reveal their identities, and in their awkward courtship Spenser explores the fitfully oscillating emotions of those who are trying to move beyond a relationship founded on power towards one which is founded upon mutual yielding. He represents the experience of love as a continual flux: Britomart knows that she should not appear to be overcome by Arthegall's submission to her. She strives to retain her appearance of heroic wrath, and fights to keep her sword arm raised; but, like Arthegall before her, she is overcome: 'Her hand fell downe, and would no longer hold | The wrathfull weapon gainst his countnance bold' (IV. vi. 27). Love is a process of oscillating supremacy, of fitful battles between the urge to conquer and the will to submit. Spenser attempts to evoke in the love of Britomart and Arthegall a form of relationship which has much in common with Chaucer's vision of love as 'a fusion which makes obedience not a matter of the execution of commands, but the spontaneous moulding of oneself to the other, so that it is no longer possible to say whose will dominates and whose is subjected'.[6] One lover achieves maisterie which they then surrender back to their partner by an act of voluntary submission. Eventually, after their mutual yielding has brought the element of power in their relationship into momentary equipoise, Britomart, Arthegall's conqueror, consents to marry him:

> At last through many vowes which forth he pour'd,
> And many othes, she yeelded her consent
> To be his loue, and take him for her Lord,
> Till they with mariage meet might finish that accord.

> (IV. vi. 41)

'Accord' is a strong term for Spenser for a treaty which is mutually agreed. In this final, vital stage of the courtship, mutual consent cancels out the battle of wills which dominated its early stages. Maisterie is renounced, after the fightful uncertainties of oscillating dominance, and replaced by 'accord' – though in the sound of that word there reverberates a memory of 'Lord'. The episode shows Spenser attempting to develop a view of love founded upon consent out of a medium which is inherently antagonistic to that ideal. And the accord of Britomart and Arthegall is brief: they separate almost at once to continue their quests.

In *The Faerie Queene* no episode is without its parodic antitype, and the courtship of Britomart and Arthegall is no exception to this rule. In Book V Arthegall does battle with another masculine woman, the amazon Radigund. She requires that before they do battle he agree

> That if I vanquishe him, he shall obay
> My law, and euer to my lore be bound,
> And so will I, if he me vanquish may.

> (V. iv. 49)

90

'With all *thy* worldly goods I thee endow', Prince Charles mistakenly said at his wedding to Lady Diana, a possible distant descendant of Spenser; and Radigund's offer has a touch of this contractual inequality: if she loses, she implies, she will be bound, not to Arthegall's, but to her own law. The fact that someone freely consents to an agreement does not guarantee the justice of what they agree to. In the fight which follows this contract Arthegall knocks Radigund down, removes her helmet for the kill, then is, a second time, prompted to yield by the spectacle of feminine beauty. Overwhelmed by the 'miracle of natures goodly grace' which is the countenance of the amazon, he 'Empierced was with pittifull regard' (V. v. 12–13). He can no longer fight, but instead 'to her mercie him submitted in plaine field' (V. v. 16):

> So was he ouercome, not ouercome,
> But to her yeelded of his owne accord.

(V. v. 17)

The episode very closely recalls the loving battle of Britomart and Arthegall, even to the point of echoing that word 'accord'; but it knocks the swaying balance of power displayed in the earlier episode out of equilibrium. Having received the submission of Arthegall, Radigund refuses to perform the reciprocal act of gracious yielding: 'Yet would she not thereto yeeld free accord, I To serue the lowly vassall of her might' (V. v. 27). The episode illustrates one way in which the Spenserian ideal of love, which involves yielding on both sides, can swing over into political dominance. Radigund's constraining love – which has deliberate and disturbing resonances of the political love elicited by Spenser's Queen – is founded on the consent of Arthegall, but does not answer that consent with her own willing submission. This power-filled love consigns the hero to prison, where he is compelled to wear woman's clothing (as Hercules was by Omphale) and to spin. The episode, we might note, explores what it is for men to agree to a contract which they then find to be unfair, and which subjects them to a woman. The poem does not contain a similar episode in which, say, Britomart discovers that she has consented to an unequal relationship with Arthegall. Indeed, at the end of the Radigund episode Britomart kills the amazon, and 'The liberty of women did repeale, I Which they had long vsurpt; and them restoring I To mens subiection, did

91

true Iustice deale' (V. vii. 42). The poem's vision is subject to the inequities of its period, which it can voice with a souring explicitness; but it is insistent on one vital point: that love works only when people consent to it, and that love can only reach equilibrium when it issues in a mutually yielding 'accord'.

The episode of Radigund takes us from the sexual politics of the poem to its view of the ideal political relations between people. Governing *The Faerie Queene* is a notion which Spenser would call 'civility'. This term is a broad one in the sixteenth century, and means far more than the very weak sense of 'politeness' which the word usually carries today. *The Discourse of Civill Life* by Spenser's friend in Ireland, Lodovic Bryskett is concerned with the virtues which make people capable of living in a *civitas*, a city or a state; and 'civility' means the moral qualities which enable people to live together. Spenser's ideal of human relations is gracious mutuality: the inferior or the conquered offers to serve his conqueror, ruler, or mistress; and the conqueror, ruler, or mistress then graciously grants freedom to the inferior. Sovereignty is ideally renounced between equals in a civil exchange. In Book II Prince Arthur rescues Guyon from the ravages of the passionate brothers Pyrochles and Cymocles. Guyon offers 'to be euer bound' (he speaks an awed half-line, II. viii. 55) to Arthur for his salvation. Arthur, however, graciously renounces his power over Guyon, and refuses to be 'bound' in his turn to accept Guyon's thanks: 'what need I Good turnes be counted, as a seruile bond, I To bind their doers, to receiue their meede?' (II. viii. 56). The two establish a gracious community, and pass on their way 'in faire accord' (II. ix. 2). Their accord is founded upon a reciprocal yielding of supremacy: Guyon submits to Arthur, who graciously renounces his control in turn. Similar relationships run through Book VI, the Legend of Courtesy, which presses for a near equivalence between courtesy and a willingness not to constrain someone whom one has saved or helped to reward one for the favour. Sir Calidore is offered by Briana the 'Castle for his paine, I And her selfe bound to him for euermore' (VI. i. 46), but the courteous knight will 'not retaine I Nor land nor fee, for hyre of his good deede' (VI. ii. 47). However, this generous picture of what it is to live in civil accord is inherently unstable: it begins in a relationship of superiority, and it depends on the two parties involved sharing a code of nobility which is founded upon renouncing claims to which they have a theoretical right. It depends upon *both* parties being 'civil'.

No problem, one might think. But what if one of the two parties engaged in such a relationship is not prepared to accept this civil exchange? There are a variety of ways in which this happens in *The Faerie Queene*. Bad knights use their physical strength simply to constrain others to obey them. The false knight Braggadocchio makes unrestrained use of his power to gain an unqualified maisterie: when Trompart falls down before him in grovelling worship, he insists that his thrall pay him homage by kissing his stirrup and by serving him for ever (II. iii. 8), and refuses to forgo his supremacy. A model of human relations which originates in a relation of power is ripe for such abuses, and Spenser is well aware of this: one of the defining characteristics of a villain is his incapacity to renounce his control over someone he has conquered. And 'villeyn', we might recall, in its earliest uses can mean 'low class', or lacking in the moral qualities and birth that make a man 'gentle' – that is, well born, mild, or 'civil'. The second instalment of the poem contains an abundance of 'villeynous', or 'cowherd', knights who have human form, but who refuse to accept the gracious mutual bonds of civility. Spenser's heroes generally attempt to render this group of adversaries subject to their law, rather than simply annihilating them. In Book II Pyrochles is killed by Prince Arthur, but only *after* he has refused to accept the supremacy of his conqueror. Consent to the rule of law is a vital element even in Book V, which many readers see as the most violent book in the poem, since much of its action consists of Arthegall and his Iron page Talus (one of the earliest and most ruthless of English robots, who speaks only once, in wonderfully jerky, robotic way: 'The tidings sad, I That I would hide, will needs, I see, be rad.' (V. vi. 10)) galloping around the world killing whoever opposes them. But Book V does carefully discriminate between the differing forms of justice required by different circumstances. The 'civil' adversary, who can accept terms, is treated very differently from the 'uncivil' adversary who will not accept terms, and who will not or cannot enter into the community of the gracious. In the earlier sections of the book Arthegall establishes his authority as a dealer of justice, not by force of arms, but by seeking the consent of both parties to his judgement:

> So ye will sweare my iudgement to abide.
> Thereto they both did franckly condiscend.
>
> (V. i. 25)

A key word here is 'franckly'. It has some of our sense of 'openly', but it also suggests that the knights yield to Arthegall's judgement 'freely'. A 'frank' man in Middle English is someone who is not bound to an overlord by ties of feudal obligation, and the term retains its overtones of aristocratic independence in Spenser. Arthegall has encountered two litigants who share his status, and who have sufficient grasp on 'civility' to accept his terms. When Arthegall attempts to resolve the dispute between Amidas and Placidas as to who owns land and treasure swept up by the sea, he again persuades the litigants to accept his authority before he makes his judgement: 'Certes your strife were easie to accord, | Would you remit it to some righteous man' (V. iv. 16) – again a voluntary accord is the enabling condition of justice. Characters who will accept the authority of a superior power are generally allowed to live in *The Faerie Queene*: Sir Crudor, who refuses to 'yeeld' love to Briana unless she gives him a mantle lined with the beards of passing knights and their ladies' hair, is eventually defeated by Sir Calidore, and 'swore to him true fealtie for aye' (VI. i. 44), with which oath of loyalty his story ends.

But there are other more problematic moments in the later books of *The Faerie Queene* when Spenser's knights graciously grant a conditional surrender. At times their assumption that their adversaries will consent to their law is shown to be hazardous. Sir Turpine oppresses wayfarers, and proves too powerful an adversary for Calepine. Arthur defeats him once; but at Blandina's request he does not kill him. In the next canto the Prince is assailed again by the unrepentent Turpine's mercenaries, whose master refuses to accept the law of his conqueror. Eventually Arthur resorts to stringing the uncivil knight up by the heels (VI. vii. 27). In the later stages of Book V, too, Arthegall repeatedly encounters creatures, who are all presented as having subhuman forms, who are unable to accept the law of civility. Adicia, the Souldan's wife, is turned into a tiger at V. viii. 49, and is exiled to the wilds for her uncivil actions. The uncatchable hairy Malengin, whose long beard and camouflaged cloak unmistakably recall the mantles and long beards (or 'glibs') of the Irish rebels, transforms himself into a fox, a bush, a bird, a stone, and

94

finally a hedgehog, in order to escape the knight of Justice (V. ix. 16–19). There is no effort to parley or to make terms with these inhuman figures; and frequently the knights of Justice unquestioningly accept the testimony of a passing dwarf or lady as to the villainy of those whom they go on to kill. The 'wicked customes' (a favourite phrase in these later books) which these creatures follow place them, in Spenser's eyes, outside the bounds of civility – or, as we might put it now, 'beyond the pale'. And that phrase is a redolent one to apply to Spenser, since it has its roots in English efforts to bring 'civility' to Ireland: the 'pale' was the area, originally fenced in, within which English jurisdiction was established. Those 'beyond the pale' are the uncivil, the brutish, the killable. As Calidore puts it, outside the limits of 'civility'

> Bloud is no blemish; for it is no blame
> To punish those, that doe deserue the same;
> But they that breake bands of ciuilitie,
> And wicked customes make, those doe defame
> Both noble armes and gentle curtesie.
>
> (VI. i. 26)

Spenser's conception of 'ciuilitie' has a radical cutting edge: repeatedly those who 'wicked customes make' are killed, and their killing does recall the argument advanced in *A Vewe of the Present State of Ireland* that the only successful means by which to eradicate Irish customs which conflict with English law is by mass extermination. By the last phases of *The Faerie Queene* Spenser sees 'ciuilitie' as a charmed circle with a continually shrinking circumference, which can only be defended either by subjecting the uncivil to the law of civility, or by exterminating those who have ineradicable 'wicked customes'. That vision is dark.

We are now in some position to take stock of the respects in which *The Faerie Queene* is an imperial poem, and of the respects in which it is not. It presents a vision of civility which is ideally founded on empowered equality between people (I deliberately do not say 'men', since women such as Britomart can enter this community as well), and which is based upon the ideal of gracious, mutual yielding. Outsiders can be admitted to this community, provided that they consent to the terms of civility. The poem's model of human relations, that is, by no means makes a simple equation between strength and authority: conquest of another knight can enable subsequent equality and accord. But the cutting edge of its vision, and an edge that is only qualified by its continual sympathetic shadowings of its virtuous characters in its images of vice, is that outside civility there are a mass of shapeless, speechless creatures who can be executed with impunity if they refuse to accept the terms offered to them by a victor, or who are represented as being inherently unable to become members of the gracious community of the civil. These people, or creatures, get killed; and, as *The Faerie Queene* continues, the process of extermination grows in urgency and unthinkingness. But, although this is the wounding side of Spenser's vision, it is vital also to recognize the qualities which soften it. Spenser, as we have seen, continually twins the good and the bad, the savage and the civil. His time in Ireland, pressing for policies which were unheeded by his Queen, gave him an affinity with the voiceless margins of the nation.[7] As we have seen, the second instalment of *The Faerie Queene* attaches a surprising imaginative weight to the wild, the savage, and the sylvan, and shows a recurrent, slightly perplexed, awareness that the ineducable outer reaches of the savage might have an energy and value of their own. Spenser's vision has many of the structures of an imperialist thinker; but it has a theoretical affection for consentful government, and an instinctive affinity for the uncontrollable energies of the savage. These features mark it as the vision of a poet of wide sympathies – whose pitiless rigour is continually checked by an emergent awareness of the limitations of power.

The episode which most completely explores the careful limitations which Spenser imposes on the idea of empire, and which also illustrates his insistence that love be founded upon consent, is the concluding episode in the tale of Marinell and Florimell, which ends Book IV. In IV. xi Florimell is captured by Proteus, the ruler of the sea, who attempts to win her love by bribes or force:

> For when as neither gifts nor graces kind
> Her constant mind could moue at all he saw,
> He thought her to compell by crueltie and awe.

> (IV. xi. 2)

Meanwhile her lover, Marinell, is invited to the marriage of the

Thames and Medway, which takes place in the halls of Proteus. Marinell hears a characteristically plaintful Spenserian voice echoing through the sea bed: 'That piteously complaind her carefull grieffe' (IV. xii. 5). The lament of Florimell does not issue in the unhappy stasis evoked in many of Spenser's earlier complaints; it is ultimately liberating. It is heard by the man who wishes to marry her, and whom she wishes to marry. Marinell begs his mother, the water nymph Cymodoce, to intervene for him to free his lady, who is given 'vnto his will' (IV. xii. 15). Cymodoce does not appeal directly to Proteus to release the maid, but to his superior, Neptune, the god of the sea. Neptune legally owns Florimell, because she was found wandering as a 'waif' ('an ownerless object' (*OED* 1)) in 'his seas imperiall' (IV. xii. 32), and orders Proteus to release her. The episode is a fascinating and a vital one: it shows Spenser's recurrent wish to subordinate one form of apparently absolute authority to another, higher form. The domineering Proteus is shown to be subordinate to a higher 'imperiall', natural, authority (Spenser also calls the sea 'imperiall' at V. iv. 19). And Neptune does not use his 'imperiall' sovereignty simply to dominate or to conquer. Instead he graciously grants a request from a suppliant Cymodoce, and acts to reverse the effects of tyrannical constraint. Marinell and Florimell *both* want to marry, and their ability to fulfil their desire depends upon the action of an imperial sovereign. In this episode Spenser does not represent an imperial authority which simply relishes its own power, or which dominates the weak: he shows it enabling the free, voluntary union of lovers. This is not a simple defence of imperialism; rather it marks an effort to describe, and to advocate, a form of imperialism which freely chooses to limit its power in order to accommodate the wishes of its subjects. The voluntary union of Florimell with Marinell issues in the kind of fecund rebirth which Spenser, from *The Shepheardes Calender* onwards, had excelled at evoking; for, once united with his love, Marinell revives:

> As withered weed through cruell winters tine,
> That feels the warmth of sunny beames reflection,
> Liftes vp his head, that did before decline
> And gins to spread his leafe before the faire sunshine.
>
> (IV. xii. 34)

The spreading expansiveness of the alexandrine here grows from the benign exercise of Neptune's imperial power. A voluntary union of lovers, with its promise of subsequent vitality, is enabled by Neptune's graciously imperial authority.

The Neptune episode is of a piece with the implicit argument of the Mutabilitie Cantos, which were printed in 1609, ten years after Spenser's death. The Cantos again evoke a universe which is made up of a hierarchy of powers, at the top of which is a natural force, 'Great Dame Nature', of supreme benignity. At the end of the trial of Mutabilitie's case, Nature gives her judgement, that all things do change, but that by doing so they 'worke their owne perfection'. Then she vanishes:

> So was the *Titaness* put downe and whist,
> And *Ioue* confirm'd in his imperiall see.
> Then was that whole assembly quite dismist,
> And *Natur's* selfe did vanish, whither no man wist.
>
> (VII. vii. 59)

This is the poem's last and most ambiguous use of the adjective 'imperiall'. It has been apparent from the entire action of the Mutabilitie Cantos that Jove's 'imperiall' power over the earth and all in it is qualified, since he is subordinate to Nature, as Proteus is subject to the higher authority of Neptune. Nature has refuted Mutabilitie's claim to rule the cosmos by arguing that change is a subordinate part of a natural process; but it is not at all clear that by doing so she has 'confirm'd' Jove 'in his imperiall see'. Rather, her judgement has established that her authority is superior to that of Jove, since she, not he, is the force deemed competent to judge the case. She also implies that characters such as Mutabilitie who think they rule the world in fact are no more than bit-part players in an all but endless process which rolls on with or without them. Jove's imperial rule seems equally tiny in comparison with Nature's own capacious sway. It also seems decidedly frail: a major element of the giantess Mutabilitie's claim to rule the world derives from her genealogy. She is descended from the Titans, from whom she claims 'thou *Ioue*, iniuriously hast held | The Heauens rule...by might' (VII. vi. 27). As one of the race of giants who predate Jove's rule, Mutabilitie has a claim to be sprung from the earth, and to be the offspring of its original ruler. In II. x, the chronicle of Britain which Arthur reads in the

House of Alma, Spenser notes that giants originally ruled Britain, until they were conquered by Brutus. The British nation, and the government of England in Ireland too, depends on the containment and conquest of earth-sprung, giant peoples. And yet, in a manner which would have been acutely disturbing to any readers of the poem who had even a basic legal training, Nature entirely fails to rebut Mutabilitie's claim to rule the world by right of heredity. This is much more than a loose end in the poem. It suggests that its vision is, in its final stages, unravelling; that Spenser cannot fully and finally cancel out from his mind the thought that native powers still own a land which an imperial rule claims to have conquered. For a colonial administrator, such a thought is almost unthinkable. It is cast aside by Nature, whose final supremacy is in keeping with the general tendency of the later parts of *The Faerie Queene* to place natural forces over human forces. In the Mutabilitie Cantos Spenser, the poet whose writings were never quite aligned with Elizabethan policy, who never quite sang from the centre of the court, constructed a final vision of authority which subordinated imperial power to a greater force – God or Nature – which invisibly rules those who mistakenly fancy themselves to be the rulers of nations. Jove's 'empire' is seen as being finally subordinate to a higher, invisible, and vital, authority, in the same way that, as we saw in Chapter 6, Diana's efforts to mutilate the Irish landscape are subordinated to the wild energy of the land. To see this vision of limited jurisdiction as a final rebuke to the aspirations of Spenser's Queen to imperial sovereignty would be to understate the magnificent duplicity of the poem's allegorical method, in which 'our wordes and our meanings meete not': it is nothing so explicit. But readers who put down the massy volume of the 1609 edition of *The Faerie Queene* with Nature's judgement ringing in their ears would do so with a sense that human empire was not the ultimate force in the universe, that beyond and above the powers of men and women were wild powers barely visible to mortal eyes.

The limitations which the poem imposes on empire, and on the empire of love, are of a piece with the overall vision of Spenser's works which has been advanced in this book. He is a poet whose urge to make, shape, and control is always, more or less consciously, limited by external forces which he knows he cannot quite command – the passing of time, the will of his Queen, the wills of other people, the poetic legacies which he inherited. I have presented him as a poet who is – generously, magnificently, and creatively – not quite in complete control of his poem. He cannot drive it in precisely the direction which he wishes it to take, since he is a mortal poet who is subject to time, to the forces of change, to history, and to his generic and linguistic inheritance. A similar slippage between a desire for control and the achievement of that desire runs through the sexual and imperial politics of the poem. Power is never quite absolute: it always encounters higher forces – Nature, Neptune, or the resistant will of another person – which, as Spenser heroically acknowledges, check its ambitions.

Appendix
The Faerie Queene: Summary

BOOK I: Contayning, the Legend of the Knight of the Red Crosse. Or of Holinesse

i   Redcrosse (RC) defeats the monster Errour. 28–55: Encounters the enchanter Archimago and mistakes the phantasm of Una for his lady.
ii RC abandons Una, kills Sansfoy and takes up with Duessa. 28–45: Encounters Fradubio, who has been turned to a tree for dallying with Duessa.
iii Una, accompanied by a lion, mistakes Archimago for RC. Archimago is defeated by Sansloy, who carries Una off.
iv RC and Duessa see the seven Deadly Sins in the House of Pride. 38–51: Duessa switches allegiance to Sansioy.
v   RC fights with and wounds Sansioy. 20–44: Duessa seeks the aid of Night to cure him. 45–53: RC leaves the House of Pride.
vi Una rescued from Sansloy by Fawns and Satires. 20–48: Satyrane rescues her from them.
vii RC defeated by the giant Orgoglio. 19–52: Una meets Arthur, who offers to rescue RC.
viii Arthur defeats Orgoglio, and strips Duessa.
ix Arthur relates his vision of Gloriana, the Faerie Queene. 21–54: RC encounters Despaire.
x   Una and RC visit the House of Holiness, where they receive instruction.
xi RC fights and eventually defeats the Dragon, with the help

of the Well of Life and the Tree of Life.

xii The people of Eden inspect the Dragon's corpse. 13–42: RC and Una are betrothed, after a last attempt by Duessa to foil them.

BOOK II: Contayning, the Legend of Sir Guyon. Or of Temperaunce

i. Guyon (G.) is beguiled by Archimago into attacking RC. 35–61: G. and his Palmer (P.) encounter Mordant, who has been killed by Acrasia, and witness the suicide of Mordant's wife Amavia.

ii The couple's child, Ruddymane, has bloody hands which will not be cleaned. 13–46: G. and P. stay with Medina and her sisters Elissa and Perissa.

iii G. and P. leave Ruddymane with Medina. 4–46: The false Knight Braggadocchio and his squire Trompart (who have stolen G.'s horse) encounter the virginal Belphoebe in the woods.

iv G. binds Furor and Occasion, and releases Phedon, who tells how he was overwhelmed by jealous rage. 37–46: The irascible knight Pyrochles goes in search of Occasion.

v G. fights Pyrochles, and releases Furor and Occasion. 26–38: Cymochles, Pyrochles's libidinous brother, is stirred up by Atin (discord) to fight G.

vi The enchantress Phaedria ensnares Cymochles and (almost) G., who leaves his Palmer. The knights fight, until Phaedria stops them. 41–51: Pyrochles dashes ablaze into the Idle Lake.

vii G. descends into the Cave of Mammon, where he resists temptations to riches, fame, and food. He faints on returning to the 'vitall aire'.

viii Pyrochles and Cymochles descend on the unconscious G. 23–56: They are killed by Arthur. G. revives.

ix G. and Arthur visit Alma's Castle, an allegorical representation of the human body.

x In the House of Alma Arthur reads a chronicle of British History, and G. a chronicle of the elves.

xi Arthur fights and eventually defeats Maleger and his crew outside the House of Alma.

xii   G. voyages to, and destroys, the Bowre of Blisse. He captures
       Acrasia.

BOOK III: Contayning, the Legend of Britomartis. Or of Chastitie

i   Guyon is defeated by an anonymous Britomart (B.) in a
       joust. 20–67: B. escapes from Malecasta in the Castle Joyous.
ii   B.'s past. 18–52: She falls in love with Arthegall after seeing
       him in a magic mirror.
iii   B.'s past continued. She and her nurse Glauce visit Merlin
       and hear a prophecy of the progeny which will arise from
       her marriage to Arthegall.
iv   B. wounds Marinell, who is nursed by his mother. 44–61:
       Arthur vainly pursues Florimell.
v   Arthur continues to seek Florimell. 13–55: His squire,
       Timias, is wounded by a Foster (forester) and meets, and
       falls in love with, Belphoebe.
vi   Description of the Garden of Adonis, introduced by an
       account of Belphoebe's and Amoret's birth from the union
       of Chrysogone and a sunbeam.
vii   Florimell flees from a witch and her son, and is pursued by a
       monster. 29–61: Satyrane defeats the monster and fights off
       the giantess Argante from the Squire of Dames.
viii   The witch makes a false Florimell, who is abducted by the
       false knight Braggadocchio. 20–43: Florimell is captured by
       Proteus. 44–52: Satyrane meets Paridell.
ix   Paridell, Satyrane, and B. gather at Malbecco's castle, where
       Helenore and Paridell exchanges œillards as he relates the
       tale of Troy, and the prehistory of Britain.
x   Malbecco chases the eloping Helenore, and is transformed
       into Gealosie.
xi   B. meets Scudamour, who has lost Amoret. 25–55: She
       enters the elaborately decorated House of Busirane.
xii   B. rescues Amoret. In 1590 version Amoret and Scudamour
       are reunited. In 1596 Scudamour has left in despair.

BOOK IV. Contayning, the Legend of Cambell and Telamond. Or of Friendship

i Duessa and Ate (Discord) whip Scudamour into a jealous fury with B.
ii Paridell and Blandamour fall out over the False Florimell. 32–54: The early life of Cambell.
iii Cambell fights Priamond, Diamond, and Triamond whose souls transmigrate. 37–52: Cambina interrupts the battle.
iv At the tournament for Florimell's girdle Cambell and Triamond excel, until the arrival of the salvage knight (Arthegall), who is in turn defeated by B.
v B. wins the tourney. The False Florimell cannot wear the girdle of Florimell. 32–46: Scudamour stays with Care.
vi Scudamour and Arthegall fight with B. 40–47: Arthegall and B. become engaged, but part at once.
vii Amoret is captured by the unnamed figure of lust, and is rescued by Timias. 36–47: Belphoebe abandons him for infidelity.
viii Timias is reconciled with Belphoebe by a dove. 19–63: Arthur rescues Æmilia and Amoret from Sclaunder, and kills Corflambo.
ix Arthur frees Amyas. Breaks up a tussle between Paridell and Britomart.
x Scudamour relates how he found Amoret in the Temple of Venus, and took her from it.
xi The marriage procession of the Thames and the Medway.
xii Marinell discovers Florimell imprisoned in Proteus's halls while he attends the marriage. 29–35: His mother Cymodoce asks Neptune to release Florimell, which he does.

BOOK V. Contayning, the Legend of Arthegall. Or of Justice

i Arthegall resolves a dispute between a squire and Sir Sangliere as to who had killed a lady.
ii Arthegall and Talus subdue Pollente and Lady Munera, who unjustly tax wayfarers. 29–54: They destroy an egalitarian giant.
iii A tournament at the wedding of Florimell and Marinell ends

in the exposure of Braggadocchio. The False Florimell melts when she meets the real Florimell.

iv   Arthegall resolves a dispute between Amidas and Bracidas as to who owns land and treasure swept up by the sea. 21–51: Arthegall tries to liberate Sir Terpine from the amazon Princess Radigund.

v   Arthegall fights, then yields to the amazon Radigund, who falls in love with him. Clarinda, her maid, woos him on her own account.

vi   B. sets out to rescue Arthegall, but is almost ensnared by the guileful Dolon.

vii   B. dreams an allegory of her union with Arthegall in the Temple of Isis. 25–45: She kills Radigund and liberates Arthegall.

viii Arthur and Arthegall kill the Souldan. 45–51: His wife, Adicia, is turned into a tiger.

ix   Arthur and Arthegall kill Malengin. 20–50: They arrive at Mercilla's court, where they see the poet Malfont nailed up by his tongue, and witness the trial of Duessa.

x   Arthur assists Belge, who is being tyrannized by Geryoneo.

xi   Arthur kills Geryoneo, and the monster that lurks beneath his altar. 36–65: Arthegall assists Sir Burbon in his battle against a rude rabblement.

xii   Arthur liberates Irena from Grantorto, and is then assailed by the howls of Envy, Detraction, and the Blattant Beast.

BOOK VI. Contayning, the Legend of S. Calidore. Or of Courtesie

i   Calidore pursues the Blattant Beast. 11–47: He defeats Crudor and Briana, who strip the hair off passing knights.

ii   Calidore sees Tristram kill a discourteous knight, and makes the wild boy his Squire. 40–48: Rescues Priscilla.

iii   Calidore lies to save Priscilla's honour. 27–51: Calepine encounters Turpine, and hides behind Serena to avoid him.

iv   Calepine and Serena are rescued by a salvage man. 17–40: Calepine rescues a baby from a bear.

v   Serena and the salvage man are met by Arthur and Timias in the wood. 34–41: In a hermitage Serena and Timias recover from the wounds of the Blattant Beast.

vi   Serena and Timias are cured by the Hermit. 17–42: Arthur overcomes, but does not kill, Turpine.

vii   Arthur finally defeats Sir Turpine, and hangs him by the heels. 28–50: Timias and Serena meet Mirabella, who is pursued by Disdaine and Scorn, who capture Timias.

viii Arthur frees Timias from Disdaine. 31–51: Serena is captured by cannibals, and is rescued from them by Calepine.

ix   Calidore meets and falls in love with Pastorella, and stops his quest for the Blattant Beast.

x   Calidore interrupts Colin Clout's vision of the Graces dancing. 39–44: Brigands carry off Pastorella.

xi   Calidore releases and revives Pastorella.

xii   Pastorella discovers her noble parentage. 22–41: Calidore binds the Blattant Beast. But not for long.

BOOK VII. Two Cantos of Mutabilitie, under the Legend of Constancie

vi   The titaness Mutabilitie claims that she, not Jove, rules the universe. 37–55: The trial is set for Arlo Hill in Ireland, about which Spenser tells the tale of Faunus and Diana.

vii   Mutabilitie puts on a pageant of the seasons and months. 57–59: Dame Nature finds that change does not rule the Universe.

viii Two stanzas of prayer to be granted 'that Sabaoths sight' at the end of time.

Notes

CHAPTER 1. THE BIOGRAPHICAL RECORD

1. Steven G. Ellis. *Tudor Ireland: Crown, Community and the Conflict of Cultures, 1470–1603* (London and New York, 1985), 266–7.
2. Ben Jonson, *Works*, ed. C. H. Herford and P. and E. Simpson (11 vols; Oxford, 1925–53), i. 137.

CHAPTER 2. A RENAISSANCE POET

1. George Puttenham, *The Arte of English Poesie*, ed. G. Willcock and A. Walker (Cambridge, 1936), 21.
2. See Ruth Samson Luborsky, 'The Allusive Presentation of *The Shepheardes Calender*', *Spenser Studies*, 1 (1980), 29–67.
3. Jonson, *Works*, viii. 618.
4. *The First Part of the Elementarie* (London, 1582), 80.
5. Puttenham, *Arte*, 145.
6. See A. C. Spearing, *Medieval to Renaissance in English Poetry* (Cambridge, 1985).

CHAPTER 3. DYNASTIC EPIC

1. See Andrew Fichter, *Poets Historical: Dynastic Epic in the Renaissance* (New Haven, Conn., 1982).

CHAPTER 4. ALLEGORICAL EPIC

1. Puttenham, *Arte*, 186.

CHAPTER 5. HEROES AND VILLAINS AND THINGS IN BETWEEN

1. Sir Philip Sidney, *An Apology for Poetry*, ed. G. Shepherd (Manchester, 1965), 125; cf. Puttenham, *Arte*, 18–19.

CHAPTER 6. WILD MEN AND WILD PLACES

1. See R. Bernheimer, *Wild Men in the Middle Ages* (Cambridge, Mass., 1952).
2. Puttenham, *Arte*, 31.
3. See further Richard Tuck, *Philosophy and Government 1572–1651* (Cambridge, 1993).

CHAPTER 7. LOVE AND EMPIRE

1. Sheila T. Cavanagh, *Wanton Eyes and Chaste Desires: Female Sexuality in The Faerie Queene* (Bloomington and Indianapolis, 1994), 2.
2. See e.g. Gary Waller, *Edmund Spenser: A Literary Life* (Basingstoke and London, 1994), esp. ch. 1, and Simon Shepherd, *Spenser* (New York and London, 1989), esp. ch. 2.
3. See the discussion in Jill Mann, *Chaucer* (Hemel Hempstead, 1991), ch. 3, 'The Surrender of *Maistrye*'.
4. Alastair Fowler, *Edmund Spenser* (Writers and their Work; Harlow, 1977), 22.
5. To Robert Markham, 1606, in *Nugae Antiquae*, ed. Thomas Park, (2 vols.; London, 1804), i. 355–6.
6. Mann, *Chaucer*, 105.
7. Patricia Coughlan, 'Ireland and Incivility in Spenser', in Coughlan (ed.), *Spenser and Ireland: An Interdisciplinary Perspective* (Cork, 1989), 70.

Select Bibliography

For full bibliographies readers are referred to A. C. Hamilton *et al.* (eds.), *The Spenser Encyclopedia* (see below). The emphasis in this very select list is on recent works which tie in with the concerns of this book, and on works which consider Spenser in relation to other authors.

WORKS BY EDMUND SPENSER

Modern Editions

The Poetical Works, ed. J. C. Smith and E. de Selincourt (3 vols.; Oxford, 1909–10). The text of this edition, which has few notes, is reproduced in Hamilton's edition of *The Faerie Queene*.

Works, ed. W. L. Renwick (4 vols.; London, 1928–34). Does not include *The Faerie Queene* and is now very dated.

The Works of Edmund Spenser: A Variorum Edition, ed. Edwin Greenlaw *et al.* (10 vols.; Baltimore, 1932–57). The standard edition. Still very useful on historical background, but cumbersome for normal use.

The Mutabilitie Cantos (1609), ed. S. P. Zitner (London, 1968). Contains helpful, if elderly, commentary.

The Faerie Queene, ed. A. C. Hamilton (Longman Annotated English Poets; London, 1977). The photocopied text is not easy to read. Full notes are helpful, though some show their age. Good bibliography up to 1977.

The Faerie Queene, ed. Thomas P. Roche, Jr. (Harmondsworth, 1978). Straightforward annotations at the back of the book, rather than on the same page.

The Yale Edition of the Shorter Poems of Edmund Spenser, ed. William A. Oram *et al.* (New Haven, Conn., and London, 1989). Contains helpful, if slightly bland, introductions and useful bibliography. The best available – some misprints, though.

Edmund Spenser's Poetry, selected and edited by H. MacLean and A. L. Prescott (3rd edn., New York and London, 1993). The best selected edition, which also includes a good sample of modern criticism.

Early Editions

A Theatre for Worldlings, Jan van der Noodt (London, 1569). Contains Spenser's translations of Du Bellay, his earliest known verse, later revised in *Complaints*.

The Shepheardes Calender. Conteyning twelve Æglogues proportionable to the twelves monethes (London, 1579). Further editions in 1580, 1586, 1591, 1597, and in folios of 1611 and 1617.

Three Proper, and Wittie, Familiar Letters with *Two Other, Very Commendable Letters* (London, 1580). Contains three letters by Spenser and two replies by Gabriel Harvey.

The Faerie Queene (London, 1590). Contains Books I–III and the Letter to Ralegh. Also includes final stanzas of Book III in which Scudamour and Amoret are united.

Daphnaïda. An Elegie upon the death of the noble and vertuous Douglas Howard, Daughter and heire of Henry Lord Howard, Viscount Byndon, and wife of Arthure Gorges Esquier (London, 1591). Reprinted with the *Hymnes*.

Complaints. Containing sundrie small Poemes of the Worlds Vanitie (London, 1591). Includes 'The Ruines of Time', 'The Teares of the Muses', 'Virgils Gnat', 'Prosopopoia, or Mother Hubberds Tale', 'Ruines of Rome: by Bellay', 'Muiopotmos: or the Fate of the Butterflie', 'Visions of the worlds vanitie', 'The Visions of Bellay', 'The Visions of Petrarch: formerly translated'.

Colin Clouts Come Home Againe (London, 1595). Also includes 'Astrophel. A Pastoral Elegie upon the death of Sir Philip Sidney', 'The Doleful Lay of Clorinda' (which may not be by Spenser), and a group of elegies on Sidney, several by poets, such as Ralegh and Bryskett, who had Irish connections.

Amoretti and Epithalamion (London, 1595). The sonnet sequence and the marriage poem are linked by a group of short-lined poems on love known as 'Anacreontics', for their similarity to the idiom of the Greek poet Anacreon.

Fowre Hymnes (London, 1596). Includes 'An Hymne in Honour of Love', 'An Hymne in Honour of Beautie', 'An Hymne of Heavenly Love', 'An Hymne of Heavenly Beautie' and *Daphnaïda*.

The Faerie Queene (1596). In two parts. The first reprints 1590 edn., less the Letter to Ralegh and with a revised version of the end of Book III. The second contains Books IV–VI.

Prothalamion or A Spousall Verse (London, 1596).

The Faerie Queene (London, 1609). Contains the Mutabilitie Cantos.

The Faerie Queene: The Shepheards Calendar: Together with the other Works of England's Arch-Poet, Edm. Spenser (London, 1611). The first folio edition of the collected poems, reprinted in 1617. These, combined with the 1609 edition of *The Faerie Queene*, mark a distinct Spenserian revival in the early Jacobean period. Giles and Phineas Fletcher, and Michael Drayton also printed markedly 'Spenserian' poems during this period.

A Vewe of the Present State of Ireland (London, 1633). The text was originally intended to be printed in 1598, but was not licensed for publication. This edition was prepared by Sir James Ware, who altered most of Spenser's harshest remarks about the Old English. The work circulated widely in MS, and Bodleian Library MS Rawlinson B478 is believed to have been prepared for publication.

The Works of that Famous English Poet, Mr Edmond Spenser (London, 1679). The first collected edition of the works in verse and prose.

The Works of Mr Edmund Spenser, ed. J. Hughes (6 vols.; London, 1715).

The Faerie Queene: A New Edition with a Glossary, and Notes Explanatory and Critical, ed. John Upton (London, 1758). Probably the greatest edition. Many of his notes are reproduced in *Variorum*, but some valuable annotations have not been absorbed into later editions.

'Lost' and Suppositious Works

These items may never have existed, but they indicate the kind of poet which Spenser wished to be thought of as being. Some may have been adapted and included in *The Faerie Queene*. Those marked (SC) are mentioned in the apparatus to *The Shepheardes Calender*. Those marked (L) are mentioned in the Spenser–Harvey correspondence. These tend to be aimed at creating a Chaucerian persona for Spenser, and to link him with the Earl of Leicester. Those marked (C) are mentioned in the printer William Ponsonby's preface to *Complaints*. They are predominantly religious, and their lack of clear parallels with any of Spenser's known works indicates they may be a printer's fantasy.

My Slomber (L)

Epithalamion Thamesis (L) (also mentioned by William Vallans in 1590, who claims to have seen a Latin version)

Dreames (SC, L, C)

Dying Pellicane (L, C)

Stemmata Dudleiana (L) (presumably a Latin genealogical poem on the lineage of Robert Dudley, Earl of Leicester)

Nine English Comoedies (L) (hard to believe that these existed; Harvey compares them to Ariosto's comedies, probably to draw Spenser away from the unprecedented task of writing an English epic,

111

towards translation of Italian comedy)
Legendes (SC)
Court of Cupide (SC)
Pageaunts (SC)
Ecclesiastes (paraphrase) (C)
Song of Songs (paraphrase) (C)
A Senights Slumber (C) (probably the same as *My Slomber*)
The Hell of Lovers (C)
The Howers of the Lord (C)
Purgatorie (C)
The Sacrifice of a Sinner (C)
The Seaven Psalms (C) (presumably the seven penitential psalms, paraphrased by, among others, Sir Thomas Wyatt)

BIOGRAPHICAL STUDIES AND REFERENCE WORKS

Cummings, R. M. (ed.), *Spenser: The Critical Heritage* (London, 1971).
Hamilton, A.C., *et al.* (eds.), *The Spenser Encyclopedia* (Toronto, Buffalo, and London, 1990). A good starting-point. Articles of variable quality (most are excellent) contain a lot of information, and there is a very full bibliography.
Judson, Alexander, *The Life of Edmund Spenser* (vol. xi of *The Works of Edmund Spenser: A Variorum Edition*) (Baltimore, 1945). Still the standard life, despite its tendency to genteel fantasy.
McNeir, W. F., and Provost, F., *Edmund Spenser: An Annotated Bibliography 1937–72* (Pittsburgh, 1975).
Maley, Willy, *A Spenser Chronology* (Basingstoke, 1994). Dry but detailed, with a tendency to overstate the Irish connection.
Osgood, C. G., *A Concordance to the Poems of Edmund Spenser* (Washington, 1915). Not complete (selected examples only of verbal modifiers, etc.), but the only one available.
Wells, W., 'Spenser Allusions in the Sixteenth and Seventeenth Centuries', *Studies in Philology*, Supplements 68 (1971) and 69 (1972). The most useful work on Spenser's reception and influence.
Whitman, C. H., *A Subject Index to the Poems of Edmund Spenser* (Washington, 1918; repr. New York, 1966). Scarce but valuable. Indexes characters, actions, and episodes.

CRITICAL WORKS

Alpers, Paul, *The Poetry of The Faerie Queene* (Princeton, 1967; repr.

Columbia, 1982). Lucid if rather dated. Still a good starting-point for the bemused.

Bennett, Josephine Waters, *The Evolution of The Faerie Queene* (Chicago, 1942). Speculations about the development of the poem are mostly unprovable, but all are of critical interest.

Berger, Harry, Jr., *Revisionary Play: Studies in the Spenserian Dynamics* (Berkeley and Los Angeles, 1988). A collection of significant essays, some slightly dated, but all worth reading.

Burrow, Colin, *Epic Romance: Homer to Milton* (Oxford, 1993). Relates Spenser to Italian and classical epic.

Canny, Nicholas P., 'Edmund Spenser and the Development of an Anglo-Irish Identity', *Yearbook of English Studies*, 23 (1983), 1–19.

Cooper, Helen, *Pastoral: Medieval into Renaissance* (Ipswich, 1977). A very clear and full account of the literary background to *The Shepheardes Calender*.

Coughlan, Patricia, (ed.), *Spenser and Ireland: An Interdisciplinary Perspective* (Cork, 1989). Good but demanding collection of essays.

Empson, William, *Seven Types of Ambiguity* (London, 1930; 3rd edn. New York, 1953), 33–4. The best two pages ever written on the Spenserian stanza.

Fichter, Andrew, *Poets Historical: Dynastic Epic in the Renaissance* (New Haven, Conn., 1982). Very good on the Italian epic background to *The Faerie Queene*.

Fletcher, Angus, *Allegory: The Theory of a Symbolic Mode* (Ithaca, NY, 1964). Although the psychoanalytical framework is not to all tastes, and not, perhaps, for all times, there are still some resonant observations here.

Fowler, Alastair, *Spenser and the Numbers of Time* (London, 1964). Everything you ever wanted to know about number symbolism in *The Faerie Queene*. And then some.

—— *Edmund Spenser* (Writers and their Work; Harlow, 1977). Still a readable introduction, although religious and political questions do not figure large in it.

Greenblatt, Stephen, *Renaissance Self-Fashioning, More to Shakespeare* (Chicago, 1980). Contains a stimulating but partial study of the colonialism of *The Faerie Queene*.

Hamilton, A. C. (ed.), *Essential Articles for the Study of Edmund Spenser* (Hamden, Conn., 1972). An elderly but still handy collection.

Helgerson, Richard, *Self-Crowned Laureates: Jonson, Spenser, Milton* (Berkeley and Los Angeles, 1983). Good on the difficulties of being a poet, and on the roles poets make for themselves in the Renaissance.

—— *Forms of Nationhood* (Chicago and London, 1992). A provoking study of the ideology of Englishness in Spenser and later writers.

Hieatt, A. Kent, *Short Time's Endless Monument: The Symbolism of the Numbers in Edmund Spenser's Epithalamion* (New York, 1960). The first and most convincing numerological analysis of Spenser.

Hough, Graham, *A Preface to The Faerie Queene* (London, 1962). Elderly, but still a readable and clear introduction.

Hume, Anthea, *Edmund Spenser: Protestant Poet* (Cambridge, 1984). Decent account of Spenser's religious position.

Johnson, Lynn Staley, *The Shepheardes Calender: An Introduction* (University Park, Pa., and London, 1990). A very good introduction, particularly strong on historical context.

Johnson, William C., *Spenser's Amoretti: Analogies of Love* (London and Toronto, 1990). The most helpful book-length study of *Amoretti*. Some numerological excesses, but mostly sensible.

Jones, H. S. V., *A Spenser Handbook* (New York, 1930). Still a useful source of information, since its author believes that information is useful.

Kermode, Frank, *Shakespeare, Spenser, Donne* (London, 1971). Tends to make Spenser more mysterious than he is, but draws attention to the Protestant background.

King, John N., *Spenser's Poetry and the Reformation Tradition* (Princeton, 1990). Shows the extent of Spenser's debt to Reformation iconography.

Lewis, C. S., *The Allegory of Love* (Oxford, 1936), 297–360. Slightly crusty, and not to be trusted on courtly love, but the sort of introduction that makes you like Spenser.

—— *Spenser's Images of Life*, ed. A. Fowler (Cambridge, 1967). Uncomplicatedly life-affirming view of Spenser.

McCabe, Richard, 'Edmund Spenser, Poet of Exile', *Proceedings of the British Academy*, 80 (1991), 73–103. A concise and pointed account of Spenser's career, with strong emphasis on Ireland.

Miller, David Lee, *The Poem's Two Bodies: The Poetics of the 1590 Faerie Queene* (Princeton, 1988). Sometimes hard going, but insightful.

Montrose, Louis Adrian, ' "Eliza, Queene of Shepheardes" ', and the Pastoral of Power', *English Literary Renaissance*, 10 (1980), 153–82.

—— ' "The Perfecte Paterne of a Poete": The Poetics of Courtship in *The Shepheardes Calender*', *Texas Studies in Language and Literature*, 21 (1979), 34–67.

—— 'Of Gentlemen and Shepherds: The Politics of Elizabethan Pastoral Form', *ELH* 50 (1983), 415–59. All three of these intriguing articles explore, from the perspective of cultural materialism, the role Spenser sought to make for himself within his culture.

Norbrook, David, *Poetry and Politics in the English Renaissance* (London, 1984). Excellent on historical and religious context.

Norhnberg, J., *The Analogy of the Faerie Queene* (Princeton, 1976). This very large book can be perplexing, but if patiently read can be rewarding.

O'Connell, Michael C., *Mirror and Veil: The Historical Dimension of Spenser's 'Faerie Queene'* (Chapel Hill, NC, 1977). Strong and readable.

Parker, Patricia, *Inescapable Romance: Studies in the Poetics of a Mode* (Princeton, 1979). A lively study of the mode of romance, which mostly wears its theory lightly and with conviction.

Patterson, Annabel, *Pastoral and Ideology: Virgil to Valerie* (Oxford, 1988). Contains an interesting chapter on Spenser and Marot.

—— *Reading between the Lines* (London, 1994). Includes a stimulating revisionary study of *The Shepheardes Calender*.

Quilligan, Maureen, *The Language of Allegory: Defining the Genre* (Ithaca, NY, 1979). Some stimulating argument about allegory, not always to be taken as gospel.

Rambuss, Richard, *Spenser's Secret Career* (Cambridge, 1993). Interesting on Spenser's early years, and on connections between secrecy and secretaryship.

Waller, Gary, *Edmund Spenser* (Basingstoke and London, 1994). Chiefly considers gender, race, and class issues in Spenser.

Whigham, Frank, *Ambition and Privilege: The Social Tropes of Elizabethan Courtesy Theory* (Berkeley and Los Angeles, 1984). Stimulating, if hostile, view of Elizabethan courtesy theory.

BACKGROUND READING

Ariosto, Ludovico, *Orlando Furioso, translated into English Heroical Verse (1591)*, trans. Sir John Harington, ed. R. McNulty (Oxford, 1972). A bouncily Byronic translation, which roughens Ariosto up, but still catches his energy. Also includes allegorical commentary.

Auerbach, Eric, 'Figura', in *Scenes from the Drama of European Literature* (repr. Manchester, 1984). Still very informative and suggestive on allegorical thinking.

Canny, Nicholas, *The Elizabethan Conquest of Ireland* (Hassocks, 1976).

Collinson, Patrick, *The Elizabethan Puritan Movement* (Oxford, 1967, repr. 1990). Excellent discussion of what it meant to be a 'puritan'.

Ellis, Steven G., *Tudor Ireland: Crown, Community and the Conflict of Cultures, 1470–1603* (London and New York, 1985). Full.

Greene, Thomas M., *The Light in Troy: Imitation and Discovery in Renaissance Poetry* (New York and London, 1982). The best book on the how and why of Renaissance imitations of past works.

Haigh, Christopher, *Elizabeth I* (London and New York, 1988). Readable and vivid portrait. Sometimes slantedly hostile to its subject.

Javitch, Daniel, *Poetry and Courtliness in Elizabethan Poetry* (Princeton, 1978). Clear and stimulating, although it may attach too much normative weight to Puttenham.

Kerrigan, John (ed.), *The Motives of Woe: Shakespeare and Female Complaint* (Oxford, 1991). Remarkably full survey of, and critical argument about, the genre of complaint.

King, John N., *English Reformation Literature: The Tudor Origins of the Protestant Tradition* (Princeton, 1982). Gives full early sixteenth-century background to Spenser's Protestant imagery.

Puttenham, George, *The Arte of English Poesie*, ed. G. D. Willcock and A. Walker (Cambridge, 1936). The fullest contemporary manual of poetics.

Sidney, Sir Philip, *An Apology for Poetry*, ed. G. Shepherd (Manchester, 1965).

Smith, G. G., (ed.), *Elizabethan Critical Essays*, (2 vols.; Oxford, 1904). Contains Puttenham's *The Arte of English Poesie* and Sidney's *Apology for Poetry*, as well as other lesser critical works with a bearing on the poetics of Spenser.

Tuck, Richard, *Philosophy and Government 1572–1651* (Cambridge, 1993). Detailed account of late sixteenth-century humanist political thought.

Tasso, Torquato, *Godfrey of Bulloigne (Gerusalemme liberata)*, trans. Edward Fairfax (1600), ed. T. M. Lea and K. Gang (Oxford, 1981). Tasso's epic translated by a follower and near contemporary of Spenser is still the best version.

—— *Discourses on the Heroic Poem*, trans. M. Cavalchini and I. Samuel (Oxford, 1973). Near contemporary account of heroic poetry.

Spearing, A. C., *Medieval to Renaissance in English Poetry* (Cambridge, 1985). Provides an account of how 'Renaissance' ideas of the dignity of poetry permeate medieval writing.

Wilson, Jean, (ed.), *Entertainments for Elizabeth* (Ipswich, 1980). A good anthology of courtly entertainments, many of which feed *The Faerie Queene*.

Index

'Areopagus', The, 4
Abraham, 49
Adonis, Garden of, 33, 48, 68–71, 87
Aesculapius, 63
Alençon, François, duc de, 13, 34
Alma, 28, 38, 45, 48, 65
Amoret, 40, 45, 46, 48, 52, 67, 68–9,
    80–1, 84, 88, 89
Archimago, 58, 60–1
Ariosto, Lodovico, 31, 33–4, 37, 41, 46,
    59
Aristotle, 56
Arthegall, 33, 34, 37–8, 43, 47, 55, 66,
    69, 71, 72, 73–4, 89–94
Arthur, 34, 35, 38–9, 50, 57–60, 65, 73–
    4, 92, 93, 94

Belphoebe, 39, 52, 64, 68–9, 88
Boiardo, Matteo Maria, 30–1
Boleyn, Anne, 68
Bonfont, 9, 53–4
Botero, Giovanni, 73
Bourbon, Henry, 50
Bowre of Blisse, 29, 44, 55–7, 60, 71
Boyle, Elizabeth, 5, 23–4, 84
Braggadocchio, 33, 88, 93
Britomart, 28, 33, 34, 36–8, 40, 47, 58,
    66, 69, 70–1, 83–4, 87–92
Brutus, 36, 99
Bryskett, Lodovic, 6, 23, 73, 92
Burghley, Lord, see Cecil,

Calepine, 28, 73, 75, 83, 94
Calidore, 9, 28, 40, 47, 48, 73–4, 76–7,
    92, 94, 95
Camden, William, 12
Care, 45, 48, 64
Cartwright, Thomas, 2–3
Cecil, Sir William, Baron Burghley, 10,
    20
Charles, Prince of Wales, 91
Chaucer, Geoffrey, 14, 18–19, 21, 62–3,
    82, 83–4, 90
Chylde, Machabyas, 5
Clifford, Anne, 1
Colin Clout, 3, 4, 9, 12, 15, 17–19, 22–3,

    25, 29, 48, 76–7, 82
Cooper, Thomas, 77

Despaire, 33, 46–7, 48, 63, 70
Devereux, Robert, Earl of Essex, 10, 25,
    73
Donne, John, 1
du Bellay, Joachim, 2, 14, 21–2
Dudley, Robert, Earl of Leicester, 3–4,
    5, 10, 11-12, 20, 22, 25, 34, 50,
    51, 72
Duessa, 49, 52–3, 57, 80, 88
Dyer, Sir Edward, 4

EK, 3, 12, 13, 14–15, 17
Elizabeth I, 5, 9, 10, 13, 34, 38, 51–3,
    60, 68, 71, 72, 78, 80, 88, 96, 99
Erasmus, Desiderius, 49, 73
Errour, 48, 49, 67, 69, 80
Essex, Earl of, see Devereux,

Fairfax, Edward, 32
False Florimell, The, 57, 61–2, 87–8
Faunus, 77–8
Florimell, 28, 34, 44, 57, 64, 72, 80, 82–
    3, 84, 87, 96–7
Fornari, Simon, 31
Fowler, Alastair, 85
Foxe, John, 49, 60

Gascoigne, George, 4, 11
Geoffrey of Monmouth, 36, 66
Gloriana, 28, 34, 57, 73, 75, 80
Greene, Robert, 11
Grey, Lord Arthur, 6
Grindal, Edmund, 13
Guyon, 28, 29, 33, 44–5, 47, 55–7, 59,
    71, 92

Harington, Sir John, 88
Harvey, Gabriel, 3–4, 9, 33
Helenore, 35–6, 47
Henry VIII, 60, 68
Hercules, 66, 91
Homer, 29–30, 59, 68

Ireland, 5–9, 22–3, 75, 77–9, 94–6, 99

James IV and I, 10, 12
Jonson, Ben, 8, 12, 14, 52
Jove, 41, 63, 98–9

Kirke, Edward, 3
Knollys, Lettice, 5

Langland, William, 43
Leicester, Earl of, see Dudley,
Lewis, C. S., 66–7
Lipsius, Justus, 73
Lownes, Matthew, 41

Malbecco, 47–8, 64, 70
Maleger, 65–6
Malengin, 73, 94–5
Malfont, see Bonfont,
Marinell, 28, 34, 64, 96–8
Marlowe, Christopher, 11
Marot, Clement, 34
Mary I, 49, 69
Mary, Queen of Scots, 10, 52–3
Medwall, Henry, 83
Mercilla, 9, 52–3
Merlin, 37–8, 69
Milton, John, 19
Montaigne, Michel de, 73
More, Sir Thomas, 7
Mulcaster, Richard, 2, 15

Nashe, Thomas, 3, 11
Neptune, 97–8, 100
Noodt, Jan van der, 2

Ovid, 45

Paridell, 35–6, 47–8
Pastorella, 73
Petrarch, Francesco, 19, 62, 84
Philip of Spain, 50
Plato, 61, 83
Ponsonby, William 17, 20, 41
Proteus, 44, 80, 83, 87, 96–8
Puttenham, George, 11, 15, 51, 54, 61, 72
Pyrochles, 63–4, 92, 93

Quintilian, 44

Radigund, 90–2
Ralegh, Sir Walter, 5, 11, 22, 52, 73
Ramée, Pierre la (Ramus), 3
Redcrosse, 28, 33, 34, 46–7, 49–50, 58,
60–1, 63, 64, 65
Roche, Maurice, Lord, 7

Satyrane, 72–3, 76, 87
Scudamour, 40, 45, 66–7, 80, 88
Serena, 72, 73, 75, 81, 83, 89
Servius, 29–30
Sidney, Sir Philip, 4, 11, 12, 20, 22, 23, 51, 61
Singleton, Hugh, 12–13
Skelton, John, 12
Smith, Sir Thomas, 6
Somerset, Elizabeth, 25
Somerset, Katherine, 25
Spencer, Lady Diana, 91
Spenser, Edmund
    Amoretti, 23, 84–6
    Colin Clouts Come Home Againe, 9, 22–3, 75
    Complaints, 5, 9, 17, 20–2
    Daphanaïda, 20
    Epithalamion, 14, 23–5, 84, 86
    Faerie Queene, The, 5, 8, 10, 17, 23, 27–100
    Fowre Hymnes, 59, 85–6
    Letter to Ralegh, 27, 28, 39, 43, 51, 53, 57
    Mutabilitie Cantos, 28, 40–2, 67, 77–9, 82, 98–100
    Prothalamion, 1, 9, 25
    Shepheardes Calender, The, 3, 4, 5, 9, 12–19, 20, 34, 63, 82, 97
    Theatre for Worldlings, A, 2, 3, 20
    Three Letters, 3–4
    Vewe of the Present State of Ireland, A, 7–9, 10, 78–9, 95
St Paul, 59
Stone, Nicholas, 1
Stubbes, John, 13

Tasso, Torquato, 32, 58–9
Throckmorton, Elizabeth, 52
Timias, 52, 64

Una, 57, 61, 72, 87

Vegius, Mapheus, 30
Vergil, Polydore, 36–7
Virgil, 12, 13, 19, 21, 29–30, 32, 35, 37–8, 58–9, 68

Walsingham, Sir Francis, 20, 22, 51
Whitgift, John, 2–3

Young, John, 5